Nineteenth-Century Scottish Rhetoric

The American Connection

**Winifred
Bryan
Horner**

Southern Illinois University Press
Carbondale and Edwardsville

Dedicated to my husband,
David Alan Horner

Library of Congress Cataloging-in-Publication Data

Horner, Winifred Bryan.
    Nineteenth-century Scottish rhetoric : the American connection /
Winifred Bryan Horner.
    p. cm.
    Includes bibliographical references and index.
    1. English language—Rhetoric—Study and teaching—Scotland—
History—19th century—Sources. 2. English philology—Study and
teaching—Scotland—History—19th century—Sources. 3. United
States—Civilization—Scottish influences—Sources. 4. Criticism—
Scotland—History—19th century—Sources. 5. Scotland—
Intellectual life—19th century—Sources. I. Title. II. Title:
19th-century Scottish rhetoric.
PE1405.S26H67   1993
808'.042'07041109034—dc20   92-7435
ISBN 0-8093-1470-3   CIP

✒ | *Contents*

CONTENTS

✍ | *Preface*

The real purpose of this study is to open up an important era, not only to American and European scholars interested in the history of rhetoric, but also to all scholars interested in intellectual history, as that history reflects and is reflected by rhetoric. The archival materials described in chapters 4, 5, and 6 indicate what is available in certain manuscripts in Scottish archives that are important to students and scholars of nineteenth- and twentieth-century rhetoric, philosophy, psychology, critical theory, composition, and English literature.

It is during the nineteenth century in Scottish universities that English literature became an academic subject, that psychology evolved as a legitimate discipline, and that criticism developed out of the ancient study of rhetoric. We are familiar with the important developments in eighteenth-century rhetoric because it was the custom during that century for the Scottish professors to publish their lectures. The lectures of George Campbell, and particularly Hugh Blair, were reprinted in the United States and widely used in the American universities during the eighteenth and nineteenth centuries. Today, they are available in the facsimile editions of the Southern Illinois University Press Series, *Landmarks in Rhetoric and Public Address*, and are familiar to students and scholars in the history of rhetoric.

The nineteenth-century Scottish rhetoricians, however, equally important in shaping English language studies, usually did not publish their lectures, and, as a result, we are largely ignorant of their important influence. There is, however, a large collection of student notes of professors' lectures in nineteenth-century Scottish manuscript collections that gives us a picture of the study of rhetoric, English literature, and criticism during this period.[1] Two factors have hindered our study of these materials: their lack of accessibility to American scholars, and the difficulty of sorting out the thread of rhetoric and English language studies in course titles, such as logic and metaphysics, logic and rhetoric, moral philosophy and logic, and rhetoric and belles lettres.

The primary purpose of this study is to make these archival materials known to scholars, so that if they wish to order copies they will have some idea of their content, or if they work with these collections in Scotland, they can more readily select useful materials without having to sort through a number of indexes under various headings, such as a professor's name, a course title, or just the heading "Lectures," where they are interspersed with numerous other course notes. Students' notes might seem an inaccurate and unlikely source of information, but they are in fact remarkably rich and reliable.

I have necessarily put the manuscripts into the appropriate social, economic, political, religious, and educational context of nineteenth-century Scotland. Without such a context, rhetoric has little meaning. In the final chapter I draw some conclusions and make connections with American rhetoric of the time and with composition and literature in the twentieth century.

In addition to these sets of student notes and printed materials from the nineteenth-century rhetoric courses in the universities, there are the Royal Commissioners' Reports, rich resources of information. A Royal Commission of Inquiry into the State of the Universities in Scotland was appointed in 1826 and issued a number of reports during the next decade. A second commission was appointed in 1858 and issued reports in 1858 and 1863. A third commission was appointed in 1876 with reports in 1878. These reports, available in the National Library of Scotland and at the individual university libraries, contain lengthy interviews with the professors on such matters as the conduct of their classes, the materials covered, the nature of the students, the method of lecturing and examination, and the awarding of prizes. Not only the state of the universities in the nineteenth century, but the reforms instituted by the Universities (Scotland) Act of 1889, are well documented in these informative reports. They are listed in the Works Cited under "Official Publications." Other rich sources of information are the university calendars, much like the university bulletins issued by American universities. These documents list the professors who have held the chairs since their establishment and contain brief accounts of the courses' contents as well as textbooks and, in some cases, sample examinations. The first calendar was issued in 1859 in Edinburgh. The course descriptions appear to vary according to the professor, and one may well doubt their authenticity based on the discrepancies between course descriptions and actual course content in our own catalogs. Some of the catalogs contain short histories of the particular universities. These calendars are readily available on the open shelves of the appropriate university libraries.

Abbreviated versions of chapters 4, 5, and 6 have appeared as articles in *Rhetoric Society Quarterly* and *Rhetoric Review*. In those publications the annotations were considerably condensed from the full versions that appear here.

✍ | *Acknowledgments*

I should like to acknowledge my colleagues in the history of rhetoric who have served as a resource for this study: Paul Bator, Linda Ferreira-Buckley, Michael Halloran, Nan Johnson, Andrea Lunsford, Tom Miller, James J. Murphy, Don Stewart, Walter Ong, and especially George Davie, whose book *The Democratic Intellect: Scotland and Her Universities in the Nineteenth Century* originally aroused my interest in nineteenth-century Scottish rhetoric and education.

Also, I should like to acknowledge the continuing support of my friends: Ian Campbell, Peter France, Linda Hughes, Mary Lago, Elaine Lawless, Joyce Middleton, Nancy Perry, Krista Ratcliffe, Kathleen Welch, Marjorie Woods. In addition, I owe much to my editors, Kenney Withers, Carol Burns, and Kathryn Koldehoff; to the many librarians who helped me at Texas Christian University and at the University of Missouri; and to the manuscript librarians in Scotland, especially Jo Currie and John V. Howard at the University of Edinburgh, Timothy Hobbs at the University of Glasgow, and Colin McLaren and Ian Beavan at the University of Aberdeen. I certainly could not have completed this work without the wonderful help of my research assistants: Sherry Booth, Kerri Barton, Betsy Ervin, Lynée Gaillet, and Shelley Aley.

I would like to give special thanks to Edward P. J. Corbett not only for his work in eighteenth-century Scottish rhetoric but also for his support and friendship.

Finally, I wish to acknowledge the National Endowment for the Humanities, the National Council of Teachers of English, the University of Edinburgh Institute for the Advancement of Studies in the Humanities, and Texas Christian University for their support of my work.

1

The Missing Link

In the literature on the history of Western rhetoric, the eighteenth and nineteenth centuries are treated as a period of decline. James L. Golden and Edward P. J. Corbett in their introduction to *The Rhetoric of Blair, Campbell, and Whately* speak of the "incipient decline" of traditional rhetoric in England. George A. Kennedy concludes his study, *Classical Rhetoric and Its Christian and Secular Tradition from Ancient to Modern Times*, with only a cursory look at the eighteenth century and Hugh Blair. James J. Murphy in an address to the International Society for the History of Rhetoric speculated about the reasons for the "decay of rhetoric" in the nineteenth and twentieth centuries (Enos and Wiethoff). Brian Vickers' fifty-five-page "Concise History of Rhetoric," in his *Classical Rhetoric in English Poetry*, accords "rhetoric of the seventeenth century and after" just six pages and in conclusion asserts that, by this time, "as a branch of literary theory, and as a creative discipline for the writer, rhetoric has disappeared . . . not just neglected but despised" (60). According to these scholars, the decline begins in the seventeenth century, decay sets in during the eighteenth century, and the demise of rhetoric in the Western world is virtually complete by the end of the nineteenth century. In addition, contemporary language scholars in both composition and literature in North America are, for the most part, either ignorant of their historical connections with rhetoric or eager to disavow them. Finally, language scholars in England and Europe are equally unaware of contemporary scholarship in the United States in rhetoric/composition.

1

The American study of written composition—what it is, how to teach it in a technological age, its connection with critical analyses of literature, and its roots in the rhetorical tradition— occupies some of the best minds in North American scholarship. Housed in English literature departments, composition theorists have amassed a large body of research on how texts are generated. With the open-admissions policy of the 1960s, they faced the awesome task of educating students from many different dialect and language backgrounds. They responded with research on how to teach writing and, lately, with research on the effects of the new technology on writing and the cognitive processes associated with it. Recent scholarship has enlarged to include the grammar of television, film, and the computer. Finally, composition scholars have sought to legitimize themselves within the hostile atmosphere of North American English literature departments by exploring their roots and their connections to the rhetorical tradition.

To deny such connections is to deny both composition's and literature's part in a full rhetoric that has its roots in the classical world and that then and now participates in the social, cultural, and political milieu of its day. In this study I should like to establish some of those connections by looking at nineteenth-century Scottish rhetoric—the missing link that forges the chain between classical rhetoric and contemporary language studies not only in literature but also in the North American composition courses— particularly as Scottish rhetoric operated within its own context, a context different from that of England but much like that of the United States during the same period.

Traditional scholars of the history of rhetoric tend to look forward from the classical period and stop with the Renaissance, seldom venturing into the eighteenth and nineteenth centuries. North American composition scholars, however, who are engaged in studies of the history of rhetoric, tend to view it backwards from the twentieth century, often stopping at the eighteenth century with Hugh Blair, George Campbell, and Richard Whately. These trends are clearly evident in the programs of the Modern Language Association, made up of traditional language scholars, and the International Society for the History of Rhetoric, which is composed largely of classicists and historians. These scholars demonstrate scant interest in rhetoric as a nineteenth- or twentieth-

2

century study. The Conference on College Composition and Communication, an annual event drawing some two thousand North American composition scholars, on the other hand, includes many sessions on eighteenth-century Scottish and nineteenth-century American rhetoric and composition but very few on classical, medieval, or Renaissance rhetoric. Nineteenth-century Scottish rhetoric is somehow lost in between and remains today largely a closed book.

When one studies the eighteenth-century Scottish tradition that had such a strong influence on research and teaching in composition and literary studies in both Scotland and the United States and the men who forged that tradition—Adam Smith, George Campbell, and Hugh Blair—one cannot help but wonder why that strong eighteenth-century Scottish tradition, the first of the new rhetorics, appears to have ended so abruptly. Where are the students of these men? What happened to the programs they built? Did they just disappear? Or did they just not matter?

I suggest that this period of nineteenth-century Scottish rhetoric does matter and is, in fact, important not only in rhetoric but also in twentieth-century education as a whole and is vital in a study of the twentieth-century American composition course. It is the link that connects classical rhetoric to English language studies in the twentieth century. More important, it is out of the eighteenth- and nineteenth-century logic, and out of the rhetoric and belles lettres courses in the Scottish universities, that English literature, critical theory, composition, and psychology evolved. Finally, it is out of the nineteenth-century northern Scottish universities and Alexander Bain that current traditional composition developed in the United States in the first part of the twentieth century. Furthermore, it is out of the southern Scottish universities, particularly Edinburgh, that English literature and belletristic composition developed. Although Bain's influence on early-twentieth-century composition courses has been acknowledged and decried, the influence of belletristic rhetoric on the North American composition course has never been acknowledged or documented. These influences are clearly evident in the rhetoric courses in the nineteenth-century Scottish universities, which are documented in this study.

Why then, if this period is important, is it so often ignored?

3

I venture several reasons. The Scottish universities went through great changes in the nineteenth century. The Scottish educational model was different from the English model, but it was well suited to the Scottish nation—its topography, its sparse and spread-out population, and the democratic spirit of its people. Yet there was intense pressure to conform to the English model.[1] Nineteenth-century Scotland was dedicated to the education of its population, many of whom at an early age came to the universities from the provinces where they had little access to education. Thomas Carlyle, a typical student of the time, walked eighty miles to the University of Edinburgh to start his education at the age of thirteen (I. Campbell, *Thomas Carlyle* 11).

Fashioned after the Italian and French models, the Scottish universities were quite different from the English institutions. They did not have compulsory entrance exams until 1889, and students were admitted when they arrived. At Aberdeen in 1827, the average age of the entering student was thirteen. At St. Andrews, Edinburgh, and Glasgow, the age was between fourteen and fifteen. The Scots were dedicated to providing their people— not only aspiring clergy but also the new upwardly mobile business and merchant class—with a philosophically based education. It was a system ideally suited to the time and place. In the English universities, on the other hand, the students were generally better prepared. At Oxford and Cambridge, rhetoric had been dropped from the curriculum, and the student had only two choices of specialization: classical studies at Oxford and mathematics at Cambridge.

Such differences between southern and northern education were seen among Britishers and some Scots as a sign of northern inferiority, a viewpoint that might well be opposed and that many Scotsmen did indeed oppose at the time—but without success. Hence, the Scottish universities were broadly criticized in both England and Scotland during the period, and many records were not considered important or worth saving. Lectures were seldom published. Nevertheless, it was at the Scottish universities that new educational avenues were explored and innovations occurred.

These changes took place at the Scottish universities rather than at their English counterparts for good reason. The Universities of Glasgow, Aberdeen, Edinburgh, and St. Andrews were based on the models of Pisa and Bologna, which had become important commercial centers in the ninth and tenth centuries. Both the Scottish universities and their Italian models strove to offer an education for merchants and men of business and a practical rhetoric was an important part of the curricula. As one nineteenth-century Scottish professor, George Jardine, put it: Scottish education is designed to allow the student "to comprehend the elements of those other branches of knowledge, upon which the investigation of science, and the successful despatch of business, are found chiefly to depend" (31). And, he continued: "We do not, in this part of the kingdom, attach to classical learning that high and almost exclusive degree of importance which is ascribed to it elsewhere" (418).

During the nineteenth century, the Scottish universities pioneered in studies that are now familiar in contemporary curricula. Newton's theories were first taught at the northern universities; and German philosophy, as well as economics and agriculture, were a regular part of the curriculum at Edinburgh and Glasgow long before they were taught at other universities. While Oxford and Cambridge were concentrating on the classics, the Scottish universities were embracing the new learning. It was within this atmosphere, appropriate for innovation and enlightenment, that the study of English literature and critical theory and the new psychological rhetoric emerged.

Innovation often takes place in just such an atmosphere, at universities that do not have a heavy investment in the status quo. Today rhetoric as a legitimate discipline in the United States is reemerging at those colleges and universities where change is possible and inviting, at institutions that have little to gain from perpetuating a system that assigns them marginal status. Also, their students are often business and technically oriented rather than aspiring scholars. Innovation is not so inviting to such schools as Stanford and Harvard within a culture that already assigns them high status. The nineteenth-century Scottish universities were the ideal nesting grounds for such changes.

The system had its defenders as well. One of the most influential in his own time was George Jardine, professor of logic and rhetoric at the University of Glasgow from 1774 to 1827. He defended the Scottish system, maintaining that the use of English

5

had made the students realize that the old system of logic and rhetoric was inappropriate for nineteenth-century students. "From the time that the lectures began to be delivered in English, the eyes of men were opened to the unsuitable nature of the subjects of which they treated; and the defects of the system . . . became everyday more striking, and called more loudly for a radical reform" (24). He continued: "Some of the classes bear evident marks of their original design, being either totally, or in part, intended for the disputes and wranglings of divines, and of little use to the lawyer or physician, and still less to the merchant and gentleman" (26–28). He concluded that "the changes which were taking place in society required a more . . . practical kind of instruction, for . . . their pupils . . . who had less time to spare for the abstract doctrines of the ancient metaphysics" (28–29). Jardine and many of his colleagues carried this practical philosophy into their classrooms. But their ideas were shared by only a few, and by the end of the nineteenth century, the Scottish universities initiated a series of "reforms" that abandoned the nineteenth-century philosophic and democratic system and resulted in one that conformed to the English university model and that was dedicated to the education of the select few. The influence of men like Jardine was felt, however, in the United States and in the British red-brick universities that developed in the late nineteenth century. In Scotland, however, the important records of their work were often lost or overlooked in the persistent call for educational "reform."

Another reason for the obscurity that cloaks nineteenth-century Scottish rhetoric is one of simple logistics. Since there were few published lectures, the materials are not available. Hence there are the eighteenth-century published lectures of John Lawson, John Ward, Thomas Sheridan, George Campbell, and, of course, the well-known lectures of Hugh Blair, which had approximately 130 editions and were used in the American colleges for at least fifty years.[2] Unfortunately, however, this practice of publishing lectures largely came to an end with the eighteenth century. If the lectures were printed, as they occasionally were for the benefit of the students, they were manuals more than books and went out of print in short order. Some of these have been lost completely and none of them has, to my knowledge, been reprinted by a contemporary press. Consequently, we have no reliable and readily

available sources, such as the Southern Illinois University land-
mark series, for the nineteenth century.

There is, however, another source of information for the
nineteenth century: the student notes from the lectures of the
professors. At first thought, these notes may appear to be unreli-
able, but such is not the case. They are highly reliable for the best
of reasons and for the worst of reasons. One reason—the best—
is that it was the custom at the Scottish universities to award prizes
in a number of classes for the best sets of student notes. These
notes are not like anything that we are accustomed to today. There
are no love notes, no song lyrics, little marginal artwork. They are
in good condition though slightly faded. Usually the handwriting
is impeccable. Most contain a title page and a table of contents.
The pages are numbered, sometimes by a later hand. The second
reason—the worst of reasons for presuming these notes to be
accurate—is that many of the professors dictated their lectures,
often failing to change them by more than a word or two over
many years. There are seven sets of student notes from the lectures
of David Masson spanning seventeen years that do not differ in
any important aspect. And one well-known Edinburgh family held
the chair of anatomy for three generations from 1720 to 1846 and
passed the family notes down from father to son for over 120 years
(*University of Edinburgh Journal* 77). This case was obviously an
extreme, and one might argue that anatomy is slow to change. For
many students, these notes were the textbooks for the class, and
accuracy was important. Some students developed a shorthand in
which they took notes (EUL Ms. Gen. 49D), while others used
phonetic spellings, a popular movement in the nineteenth century
(GUL MS. Gen. 700).[3] Some of these prize-winning sets of notes
were immediately placed in the appropriate university library by
the student or the professor. Some have been stored and are only
now coming to light. Because of the custom of awarding prizes,
these notes have been preserved; and because of the unfortunate
custom of "dictates," it can be safely assumed that they are fairly
accurate representations of the lectures.

Unfortunately, these student notes are still largely inaccessi-
ble. First, even those notes that have found their way into the
Scottish libraries are available only in manuscript form. One must
go to Scotland to see them and read them—a considerable expendi-

7

ture of time and effort, particularly for North American scholars. In fact, some of the notes are useless—hard to read or badly damaged. Second, the search through these notes to find the thread of rhetoric is not as simple as one might expect because of the shifting terminology in course titles, which often appear to have little to do with course content. Philosophy and a new term, *psychology*, are used almost synonymously. *Pneumatology* is the early term for what we would now call psychology. There is no clear-cut terminology, and one searches through courses with such various words in their titles as *logic, moral philosophy, metaphysics, belles lettres, rhetoric,* and *English literature* to find the thread. When rhetoric disappears in one course it turns up in another, and the definition of logic may include or exclude rhetoric depending often on the whim of an individual professor. Courses vary, professors vary, and terminology varies.

By the nineteenth century, after two thousand years within the Latin tradition, rhetoric had acquired a terminology with disastrous connotations. The modern derivatives from the original Greek and Latin words—*sophistry, hypocrisy, elocution,* even *rhetoric,* itself—are eloquent testimony to this fact. In the eighteenth and nineteenth centuries, education changed its language from Latin to the vernaculars, and rhetoric emerged at the Scottish universities with a new English vocabulary less burdened with old connotations. If René Descartes changed the way of looking at the world, then John Locke and the Scottish philosophers and rhetoricians— Thomas Reid, George Campbell, James Beattie, and Alexander Gerard—changed the way of talking about it, a further confusion to the scholar of rhetoric. Testimony to this truth is that most lecturers started their courses by defining or redefining rhetoric and logic.

Because of the inaccessibility of the primary materials and the changing vocabulary, we retain the impression that the nineteenth century is a break in the tradition and a sharp departure from classical rhetoric rather than a logical transition. A study of the materials available to us from this period (the students' notes) demonstrates two movements that connect rather than disrupt the thread. The first movement that starts in the eighteenth century and continues in the nineteenth century is the movement from a generative to an interpretive rhetoric, as professors move from

8

rhetoric to belles lettres and from examples in Greek and Latin literature to ones in English literature. It is out of this movement that the academic discipline of English literature evolves. The second movement is the reestablishment of rhetoric's ancient connection with psychology in the move from a philosophic to a psychological rhetoric and the rise of psychology itself as an academic discipline. This movement represents a shift from a philosophical search for values and reality through dialectics to a psychological search for an understanding of mind and human behavior by observational rather than speculative means. Psychology emerges as the appropriate partner to rhetoric in a period of science where truth depends on observable physical phenomena rather than on dialectics and philosophical disputation.

The concepts of literature and psychology as we know them now simply did not exist prior to the eighteenth century. The development of the words themselves was an eighteenth-century phenomenon. The first occurrence of the word *literature* in the *Oxford English Dictionary* in our modern sense of "writing which has claim to consideration on the grounds of beauty of form or emotional effect" or "the writing of a certain area or period" was in 1812, and the editors of the dictionary noted that "this sense is of very recent emergence in both France and England." Also, the first occurrence of the word *psychology* was in the late seventeenth century and the second was in 1749 from David Hartley's *Observations on Man, His Frame, His Duty, and His Expectations*, in which he defined it as "the theory of the Human Mind."

The initial movement from rhetoric toward belles lettres and literary criticism is clearly set forth in students' notes from Robert Watson's lectures at St. Andrews in 1764 in which he defines rhetoric and criticism.

Rhetoric is the art which delivers rules for the excellence and beauty of discourse. By the rules of rhetorick or fine writing else is meant but observations concerning the most excellent and useful; it is not proposed to deliver them in the form of rules, but in the form of general Criticisms illustrated by passages from Authors, so what follows therefore may be given either the name of rhetoric

9

or of Criticism; for if it deserve the name of the one it
will deserve the other also. (EUL MS. Dc. 6.50/2)

This change is most evident in the widely influential lectures of
Hugh Blair, first delivered in the city of Edinburgh. They proved
so popular that in 1760 he was appointed to the newly established
Regius Professorship of Rhetoric and Belles Lettres. Blair held the
chair for twenty-four years and published his lectures in 1783.
Their popularity was immense in both Britain and the United
States. They were used at Yale and Williams until 1850 and until
1880 at Notre Dame (Guthrie 61). Through them, rhetoric's
connection with criticism and belles lettres was firmly established.
Through them, the professorships of English in Scotland and the
United States developed in the nineteenth century.

William Edmondstoune Aytoun, the first formally titled professor of English language and literature held the Regius chair at
Edinburgh from 1845 to 1865.[4] His course covered the whole
range of English literature in roughly chronological order, but
he also included lectures on Roman literature, Early European
literature, ballads, poetry, and language, style, and versification.
In his report to the Royal Commission of 1858, he stated that he
did not believe in instruction in formal rhetoric because "I believe
the ancient systems to be unsuited to the circumstances of our
time" (NLS MS 4913, fol. 29 v). In his introductory lecture, he
stated: "I would much rather sit in this chair as Professor of
English Language and Literature, than as Professor of Rhetoric
and Belles Lettres." In the manuscript, the line "I would much
rather" has been erased and "I am delighted to sit in this chair"
is substituted, a change obviously made after his appointment
(NLS MS 4897, fol. 35). Largely because of Aytoun's popularity
and influence, the Royal Commission of 1861 recommended that
the study of English literature be added to the curriculum of all
four of the Scottish universities, but since none of them had at
that time such a course, English was assigned to the professor of
logic—the historic home of rhetoric. It was out of these nineteenth-century Scottish courses and these professorships that the
powerful departments of English developed in the twentieth
century.

At these same nineteenth-century Scottish universities, rhetoric reestablished its connection with psychology, which in that period developed as an academic discipline. The influence of the Scottish philosophers on eighteenth-century rhetorical invention has been well documented in our scholarly literature (e.g., Howell; Ehninger). Douglas Ehninger maintains that eighteenth-century rhetoric stands as the great watershed that divides the old from the new rhetorical theory. He recognized with other scholars that everything that we read before that period seems unfamiliar, while much that we read in the eighteenth and nineteenth century has the ring of modernity. If everything after Descartes is new, then it was Locke who provided the new vocabulary for the new rhetoric. If what we read in eighteenth- and nineteenth-century rhetoric has the ring of modernity, it is the vocabulary as much as the concepts that is modern. It is this new philosophy with its new vocabulary that invades the field of rhetoric, takes over the classical concept of *inventio*, separates logic from its traditional rhetorical base, and emerges as the new psychology.

The beginnings of this development in the eighteenth century are documented in the published lectures from this period. The new rhetoric of the eighteenth century as it was altered by the Scottish philosophy of common sense, faculty psychology, and associationism can be clearly traced in these materials.

The continuing trend in the nineteenth century must be traced in the students' notes, but it is far from clear because of the vocabulary. The confusing terminology is strikingly demonstrated by the 1884 title page of Alexander Bain's book, *Mental and Moral Science, a Compendium of Psychology and Ethics*. At that time, he was the professor of logic. In a moral philosophy course, Dugald Stewart covered such diverse topics as consciousness, perception, memory, the association of ideas, appetites, desires, affections, duties with respect to the deity, to our fellow man, and to ourselves. It would take half a dozen modern professors each in a specialized department to do what most eighteenth-century professors did in their courses in moral philosophy or logic (Howell 413). It is through this labyrinth of terminology and course lectures that one sees the emergence of the new psychology and logic, as well as English composition, literature, and criticism.

Professor Jardine, who provides us with one of the best sources in his published book *Outlines of Philosophical Education*,

11

describes the subjects of the lectures for his logic course, which he substitutes for the ancient logic and metaphysics. His primary subject matter, he asserts, is mental science, the study of the mind, which includes lectures on perception, improvement of memory, imagination, judging and reasoning, the Baconian method of induction, improvement of the powers of genius, and six lectures on the improvement of the powers of taste. This logic course was the first course that students encountered in their philosophy curriculum at the University of Glasgow, and it was followed the next year by a course in moral philosophy, which covered much of the same ground (Jardine 21). Although course titles differ, the content of the courses in moral philosophy, logic, and rhetoric are almost indistinguishable at the beginning of the nineteenth century. In 1829, the moral philosophy course is described in the University of Glasgow Calendar of 1829 as "the objective study of the mind."[5] By the end of the century, the new philosophy is replacing the old philosophy of logic and metaphysics.

Nineteenth-century scholars were fascinated with this study of the mind, and the new psychology invaded thinking in the areas of logic, rhetoric, belles lettres, criticism, taste, ethics, and morals. The *Oxford English Dictionary* lists some fifty compounds with the *psycho-* prefix: psycho-auditory, psychoblast, psycho-ethical, psychoguesic (having to do with the mental perception of taste), psychosomatic, and psycho-optic—all of them originating in the nineteenth century and many of them dropping from use soon after, fortunately. For the nineteenth century, logic became not the study of inductive or deductive inferences but the study of the workings of the human mind.

Psychology emerges even more strongly at the northern University of Aberdeen in the eighteenth and nineteenth centuries. Thomas Reid, the commonsense philosopher, attended Marischal College, the liberal arts precursor of Aberdeen between 1722 and 1726, and remained there as librarian for four years from 1733 to 1737. In 1751 he was appointed to a lectureship at King's College, Aberdeen, where he lectured on logic, ethics, physics, and mathematics for thirteen years. In 1758 he, together with George Campbell, who was principal of Marischal College from 1759 to 1796, founded the Aberdeen Philosophical Society. At the meetings of the society, Reid presented papers from his famous "An Enquiry into the Human Mind, on the Principles of Common Sense," and Campbell presented excerpts from his *Philosophy of Rhetoric*. These men exerted a powerful effect on each other and on the community of scholars at Aberdeen. Alexander Gerard wrote his "Essay on Taste" while teaching moral philosophy at Aberdeen, and William Duncan, the author of *Elements of Logic*, was appointed professor of natural philosophy at Marischal the same year Gerard was appointed—1753.

The influence of this philosophy on the emerging psychology in the nineteenth century is evident in the descriptions of the logic courses from the University of Aberdeen Calendar after King's College and Marischal were combined in 1860. The 1864 description lists the subjects of the logic course as "the Intellectual Powers of the Mind, including the Senses; and the principles of logic, embracing the Syllogism, Induction, and Definition." This course was taught by Alexander Bain, and under him the new psychology appears firmly established in his description of the logic course in the 1884 calendar. Here, "The subjects [of the course] are—the Principles of Logic, embracing the Logic of Consistency, and the Logic of Scientific Investigation and Inference; and the PSYCHOLOGY OF KNOWLEDGE, including the senses." (The uppercase emphasis is Bain's.) Curiously, through student notes and reminiscences, we learn that Bain's psychology course was as popular, as widely attended, and as fondly remembered as his course in rhetoric and grammar was unpopular. The grammar course was one that he felt his students from the sparsely populated northern provinces needed badly, and its prescriptive emphasis on correctness marks it as a forerunner of the early freshman composition courses—the rhetoric of correctness—of the late nineteenth and early twentieth centuries in the United States.

One of the most quoted truisms about psychology is that it has a long past, if only a short history. A look at the terminology suggests a short history, but a look at Aristotle and Plato suggests the long past. Book Two of Aristotle's *Rhetoric* must surely be included as part of psychology's long past. Plato defined oratorical ability as *psychagogia*, the art of enchanting the soul. In the nineteenth century, logic shifts from a study of valid inferences to a study of the mind, the new psychology, that connects itself to rhetoric, and by the end of the century both logic and psychology become subjects in their own right.

The rhetoric of the nineteenth century abandoned the logical proofs of the syllogism, the enthymeme, and the topics, but came, on the other hand, full circle in returning to the ethos and pathos of traditional rhetoric. Aristotle's Book Two is an outdated psychology manual, and the psychology of the nineteenth century seems equally quaint in the light of modern empirical studies. But the concept of the wedding between psychology and rhetoric is as valid in the nineteenth century as it was for Aristotle and Plato. As such, it falls comfortably within the classical tradition and in addition points forward to the cognitive rhetorics of the twentieth-century North American composition scholars.

In sorting through the maze of student notes and confusing terminology of nineteenth-century Scottish rhetoric, one begins to see the thread that links rhetoric's past to its present. One sees the shift from a generative rhetoric to an analytic rhetoric in belles lettres and criticism and from a study of the classics to a study of vernacular literature. As all of these forces interact, the result in the English-speaking countries is the formation of the English literature courses and the rise of departments of English in the twentieth century—reestablishing the classical connection between rhetoric and poetics. In North America, one sees the development of large composition programs within English departments marked by a rhetoric of correctness in the first half of the twentieth century, under the influence of Alexander Bain, and by belletristic composition in the second half of the century, strongly influenced by Scottish belletristic rhetoric. The development of belletristic composition is reinforced by its long association with literature within the rhetorical tradition and further reinforced by political and economic factors within the North American academy.

All of these developments can be traced quite clearly in the lecture notes of the nineteenth-century Scottish professors contained in this study. These materials enlighten and support work in language studies for the twentieth century. They provide the missing link that sees our present in the context of rhetoric's long history. This study places these notes within the context of

14

nineteenth-century Scotland and provides detailed annotations of their contents. In doing so, it makes them available to traditional scholars of rhetoric, as well as to North American composition scholars who are looking back to the more recent history of rhetoric to discover their roots.

🖎 | 2

The Background

Scottish independence and democracy and the shape of its educational system are derived in no small part from the ruggedness and remoteness of the land. Lying north of England and Ireland, Scotland is penetrated by a series of oceanic inlets, called *firths*, and surrounded by islands. The landscape is dotted with lakes, called *lochs*, pronounced with the glottal fricative that is still preserved in the Scottish tongue. Scotland is on the same latitude as Newfoundland and Hudson Bay, but in spite of its northerly location, its climate is remarkably mild, mitigated by the surrounding ocean and the protective winds. Nevertheless, fierce winds and rain can make a mild climate daunting.

The terrain and climate of Scotland strongly influenced the development of the schools and universities. The northern universities, as we shall see, were formed to serve a people who were isolated and poor but who wanted desperately to be educated and surmounted great odds to secure that goal. The southern universities, particularly Edinburgh, served a large urban population, many of whom attended the university lectures for entertainment and edification.

The 1707 Act of Union, combining the parliaments of Scotland and England, brought about great prosperity because Scotland was no longer excluded from profitable overseas trade by the Navigation Acts or hampered by tariffs in its trade with England. Glasgow merchants, for example, accumulated great fortunes in the eighteenth century from the trade of tobacco with North America and of beef cattle with England. The developing merchant class were eager for education but demanded a more practical curriculum than the traditional classical one. In the healthy economy, a thriving intellectual activity developed as the literati explored the "science of man" in the Scottish Enlightenment. Jacobitism, the attempt to restore the Stuarts to the throne, lost support by the mid-eighteenth century after a number of futile skirmishes, and Scotland settled down to its newfound prosperity. At the 1707 Act of Union, Scotland gained prosperity, lost its independent parliament, but retained its legal system, its national church, and, most importantly, its system of education.

Scotland's legal system was based on the civilian law of the Continent rather than on the English common law. Scotland also kept its own judicature, which did not allow for appeal to England. The National Church of Scotland, strongly Calvinistic in spirit and Presbyterian in governance, was formally constituted in 1560, and its history is marked by dissension. At the union, the Scottish Parliament passed an act preserving their Presbyterian form of governance, and the English Parliament passed a similar act preserving the status of the Church of England. In the eighteenth century, the Scottish moderates took control of the General Assembly of the church. Their more rational morality appealed to the intelligentsia of the universities and to the newly wealthy merchants who felt more comfortable with the relaxed religious strictures.

At the time of the union, England had two universities, and Scotland had four well-established ones. Over the centuries, the Scots had developed an educational system that was in fact superior to England's in many ways and was admirably suited for their people. Scotland's universities were highly respected on the Continent and in England, and the influence of their graduates in the establishment of universities in the New World has been well documented (e.g., Anderson). University historians speak of the "democratic myth" associated with Scottish education, which R. D. Anderson explains not as "something false" but as an "idealization and distillation of a complex reality, a belief which influences history by interacting with other forces and pressures, ruling out some developments as inconsistent with the national tradition, and shaping the form in which the institutions inherited from the past are allowed to change" (*Education* 1). This myth, for which Anderson identifies several parts, has been central to the Scottish educational tradition. To begin with, there was the idea of universality, in that education was to be accessible to everyone no matter how geographically isolated they were. Thus developed the "school in every parish." Also, education was to be available to all comers whatever their economic background. Thus developed the partly true, partly romanticized "lad o' pairts"—the poor but bright student who was not to be denied access to education. Another part of the myth, according to Anderson, was that schools should be places where "all social classes rubbed shoulders" (*Education* 2). The myth did in fact shape reality. Lawrence Stone quotes figures showing that, as late as the early nineteenth century, the University of Glasgow drew one-third of its students from the working class, while Cambridge drew none (136). Supporting the myth was the strong belief that education was not only everyone's right but also everyone's responsibility. Thus, in contrast to England, Scotland early developed a national school system that encompassed parish schools in the rural areas, burgh schools in the villages, and the early universities that furthered the education of those students who wished to go on. Consequently, well into the nineteenth century, the universities, especially those in the north, took the students when they arrived and continued their education where the parish or burgh school had left off.

Historians generally regard the *First Book of Discipline* in 1560 as the "founding charter" of Scottish education. This document outlined a national system of education that sought to establish in every parish a school, which was to be maintained by the landowners and was to be open to both boys and girls. The students were to learn the "shorter Catechism," but the main business of these schools was to teach reading and writing. The schoolmaster was also expected to teach Latin, mathematics, and possibly Greek for those students who wished to attend university, thus establishing "the direct relationship between the parish schools and the universities" whereby "the universities came down to meet the parish schools by admitting boys at fifteen or even younger and by providing elementary instruction in the 'junior classes' which began the college course" (R. D. Anderson, *Education* 3–4).

The History of Scottish Education

The history of Scottish education is usually divided into three periods (e.g., Morgan; Kerr). The first is characterized by

18

the founding of the medieval universities under the patronage of the Catholic church. The second period begins with the Reformation in the sixteenth century and is marked by strong support for education at all levels by the presbyteries. In both of these early periods, the church dominates, but in the last period, from the Revolution of 1688 onward, the schools and universities move rapidly from ecclesiastical to state control.

The three oldest Scottish universities were founded in the fifteenth century. At the time, relations with England and France were strained, and the Scottish students who attended universities in these countries encountered hostility from their masters and from their fellow students. Consequently, St. Andrews, the oldest of the universities, was founded by papal bull in 1411, and its establishment was celebrated with great festivity by the people of the town. Soon after, in 1450, William Turnbull, a graduate of St. Andrews, obtained a papal bull to establish the University of Glasgow. It barely managed to survive for the next two centuries, but it was revived by Andrew Melville in the latter half of the sixteenth century. Since that time, it has continued to grow as the town itself has expanded and flourished. Aberdeen was the last of the medieval institutions to be founded. In 1494, the local bishop, a graduate of Glasgow, obtained a papal bull for the purpose of "the promoting of civilization among the Highland clergy" (qtd. in Mountford 11), and in 1505 St. Mary's College, later King's, was established. Marischal College was founded in 1593 by Presbyterian interests, and the colleges existed side by side until they were united as the University of Aberdeen in 1860. Edinburgh, the last of the four universities founded before the union, in contrast to the other institutions, owed nothing to church authority. It was founded as the "tounis colledge" in 1583 by the town council who until the nineteenth-century reforms appointed all professors and determined all academic decisions.

In the medieval universities, first-year students were called bejani from the French *bec-jaune*, meaning a nestling. Second-year students were semi-bejani, while third-year students who were approaching graduation, when they would be crowned with a laurel wreath, were called baccalaurei. Fourth-year students were named magistrands. All instructors in these early universities were members of the clergy, and the regenting system was in full force. The regents carried a student through the full three or four years, teaching all the subjects and conducting all exams. In addition, they lived at the college and were required to check their students' rooms at night and arouse them at dawn for lessons. There was usually no salary for this thankless position, the regents depending on student fees for their living (Morgan 58), so it is no surprise that there was some difficulty in finding persons for these positions. Nevertheless, the regenting system persisted at the Scottish universities well into the eighteenth century. It was abandoned at all of the universities by the middle of that century except at King's College.

Four degrees, similar to the European degrees, were awarded at these early universities. The bachelor's (B.A.) was awarded after the candidate passed the exams at the end of two years. The licentiate was an earned license to teach in any university in Europe. The master's (M.A.) was awarded after four years, and the doctorate, the highest degree of the three, was originally awarded with the idea that the holder would teach at the university. This requirement, however, could often be waived through the payment of a small fine (Morgan 62). The candidate for a degree was examined orally, sitting "upon ye blak stane." St. Andrews provided a piece of local rock painted black; Glasgow offered a piece of black marble for the candidate to sit on for the traditional so-called Blackstone examinations (Morgan 60).

All lectures were in Latin, dictated or "dited" by the professor and recorded word for word by the student. These dictates substituted for textbooks, which were not available at all until the end of the fifteenth century and were scarce and expensive up to the nineteenth century. The curriculum was based on the classics, and rhetoric, an important part of the curriculum, served as the culmination of the students' education. Alexander Morgan points out that the Greek form of disputation "seemed to suit the temperament of the people, for it increased as time went on, and may have helped to develop what is often regarded as a feature of the Scottish character—'the scholastick itch of disputing all things'" (59).

The Reformation introduced a new period in Scottish education. By the sixteenth century, French and Catholic influences had ceased to be important. The new Protestant church, under the leadership of John Knox through his *Book of Discipline,* guided the decisions of educational leaders until a state system was set up three hundred years later. The writers of this document "had no truck with distinctions between the rich and the poor" (Findlay 12). In addition, promotion from one stage to the next was based on ability—the root of the Scottish tradition of "democratic meritocracy." As Ian R. Findlay points out:

> The universities' part in this scheme was to provide a very broad, general upper 'secondary' education before the real university course began at the age of nineteen. In later centuries the bright scholar did in fact go straight from parish school (or via a short grammar-school course) to university in his mid-teens. Traditions of postponement of specialisation in the Scottish school stem from this pattern. (12)

Important innovations were introduced into the Scottish universities by Andrew Melville, who accepted the principalship at Glasgow in 1574. He set out to establish a curriculum that was adopted by the other universities and that lasted well into the nineteenth century. He obtained a new charter, the *Nova Erectio et Fundatio,* for the university, which outlined among other things, a curriculum that was refined in a later statute. As summarized by Morgan, it stated,

> "In the first class, from 1st October to 1st March, the principles of Greek Grammar were to be taught and illustrated by reading Isocrates, Lysias, and Libanius. From the latter date till 1st September the principles of Eloquence were to be explained from the *Rhetoric* of Taleus, and the various kinds of style were to be exemplified by reading Cicero, Demosthenes, Homer, Aristophanes, epigrammatic Greek, &c.
> "In the second class, for half the year, the art of Rhetoric was to be fully treated by studying Aristotle and Cicero's *de Oratore,* with the applications of the rules in Demosthenes, Sophocles, and Pindar; in the other half-year the principles of Invention and Disposition were to be briefly and accurately unfolded from the *Dialectic* of

21

Petrus Ramus, and illustrated from Plato, Plutarch, Cicero's *de Finibus,* and Tusculan Questions.
  "In the third class, the subjects were to be first
Arithmetic, Geometry, and other branches of Mathemat-
ics; and after that Aristotle's *Logic, Ethics,* and *Politics,* Cicero's *de Officiis,* and selections of Plato's *Dialogues.*
  "In the fourth class were to be studied Aristotle's
Physics, the Doctrine of the Sphere, and Cosmography;
also an introduction to Universal History, and the principles of the Hebrew tongue." (Qtd. in Morgan 65)

The other Scottish universities adopted many of Melville's
reforms; and in 1642, representatives from the four universities
met to try to establish a uniform curriculum in the arts and to
institute an entrance exam, changes that did not actually take place
until the nineteenth century. In 1647, a commission representing
the universities met and made a number of new recommendations,
including one that suggested that "the unprofitable and noxious
paines in writeing be shunned . . . and that the Regents spend not
too much time in dyteing of thair notts" (qtd. in Morgan 68), a
suggestion that if carried out would have made this study impossible and left the rhetoric of the nineteenth-century universities a
mystery.
  The period that began after the Revolution of 1688 ushered
in an era of great reform that began in the seventeenth century
but did not actually accomplish much until well into the nineteenth
century, the period that concerns us in this study. A commission
appointed in 1690 issued a series of regulations, among which,
once again, were suggestions about an entrance exam, as well as a
firm recommendation that "the ordinary custome of dictating and
writing of notes in the classes be discharged from and after the
month of October 1696" (qtd. in Morgan 71). Three hundred
years later, however, faculty were still dictating and students were
still writing notes. In spite of many well-intentioned recommendations, the universities, after the abolition of regenting, did not
change much until the reforms of the nineteenth century. During
the eighteenth century, however, the Enlightenment introduced a
period of great intellectual vitality, a movement closely connected

with the universities and led by a group of literary men called the moderate literati of Edinburgh.

In furnishing the background for a study of nineteenth-century Scottish rhetoric, it is difficult to consider the universities without considering the Enlightenment; and it is impossible to consider the study of rhetoric without considering the cultural milieu of eighteenth-century Scotland in which it was embedded.

The Eighteenth-Century Enlightenment

The eighteenth century was a period of great economic growth and new opportunity in Scotland.[1] Having entered into the union with England and survived the great famine of 1696–1703, the Scots turned to the more secular pursuit of making money. They "magnified the virtues of thrift, abstinence, and hard work into a kind of piety" exemplified by the fact that the church-issued copies of the *Shorter Catechism* had the multiplication tables printed on the back (Mackie 288). But with this tradition, instilled by centuries of struggling under adverse conditions, the Scots took full advantage of their new opportunities and thrived.

The eighteenth century was also a period of transition as the agricultural population migrated to the cities in large numbers. Industrialization was rapid. Scotland changed over the century from a poor agricultural society to a relatively industrialized one with a great increase in population. Agricultural reforms were brought about by the clan chiefs and by large-scale landowners, who were struggling to get more income from their holdings. They were spurred on in no small part by the more productive methods of the English, which they had ample opportunity to observe in their trips to and from parliamentary sessions in London. In the nineteenth century, the Scottish universities incorporated instruction in the new agriculture into their curriculum, the first institutions to do so. As they developed their roads and waterways into navigable streams, industry and commerce increased. Fisheries and coal, iron, and lead mines developed, and the manufacture of wool products was set up. The eighteenth century, particularly after the American Revolution, was a period of great growth and prosperity for the Scots.

It was also a period of upward mobility, and "good English"

became a rung on the ladder. Although English was in fact the language of Scotland, it differed markedly from the London standard. Much of Scottish education since the 1707 Act of Union concentrated on the perceived need to eliminate Scottish "rusticisms" and to learn the London standard. With economic stability established, the large and powerful merchant class and those aspiring to better themselves saw education in general and language in particular as one of the ways to move up. In response, the schoolteachers and grammarians, with a strong belief in rationality and rules, set out to standardize the language, firm in the beliefs that change was a sign of deterioration and that Latin was the standard by which all languages should be measured.

During this century, the Scots remained highly religious, comfortably combining their ecclesiastical and worldly pursuits. While the Roman Catholics and the Anglicans decreased in number, the Scottish church increased, but it was plagued during the century by a number of dissatisfied groups from within. In the face of threats of secession from all sides, the moderates managed to take control of the General Assembly. This group, composed largely of literary men and professors at the universities, included many of the names most familiar to scholars of rhetoric and literature. Hugh Blair was a representative to the General Assembly nine times; George Campbell, eight times; Alexander Carlyle, seventeen times; and William Robertson, principal of the University of Edinburgh, twenty-one times (Sher 128). Richard B. Sher characterizes the attitudes of these moderate literati, who dominated not only the General Assembly but also the literary and university life of Scotland in the Enlightenment, as follows:

> "Literati" signifies men of arts and letters who adhered to a broad body of "enlightened" values and principles held in common by European and American *philosophes*. These included a love of learning and virtue; a faith in reason and science; a dedication to humanism and humanitarianism; a style of civilized urbanity and polite cosmopolitanism; a preference for social order and stability; a respect for hard work and material improvement; an attraction to certain types of worldly pleasures and amusements; a taste for classical serenity tempered by sentimen-

talism; a distrust of religious enthusiasm and superstition;
an aversion to slavery, torture, and other forms of inhu-
manity; a commitment to religious tolerance and freedom
of expression; and at least a modicum of optimism about
the human prospect if people would take the trouble to
abide by these principles and cultivate their gardens as
best they can. By the term "literati," then, I mean not
merely men of letters but men of the Enlightenment. (8)

The Enlightenment was a period of great advances in mathematics,
medicine, and the physical sciences. In chemistry, there was Joseph
Black; in geology, there was James Hutton, a contemporary and
colleague of Black; together they discovered latent and specific
heat and laid the foundations for the modern study of geology.
Agricultural advances resulted in improved machinery and the idea
that the natural resources of the land might not last forever and
must be preserved through such programs as crop rotation and
fertilizer. Agricultural societies to spread new information became
common throughout Scotland. Philosophy thrived under the influence of Francis Hutcheson, Thomas Reid, and David Hume,
founders of the Scottish school of common sense, which was to
have so much influence on the rhetoric of the eighteenth and
nineteenth centuries. The Enlightenment was a time of religious
tolerance and moderation, great intellectual activity, and concern
for practical improvements based largely on the study of human
beings and their place in the natural world and in society. All of
the men involved in the Enlightenment were deeply concerned
with morality and its place in their government, in their schools
and universities, and in their own lives. It was a broadly cultural
movement rather than a narrowly intellectual one. As moderates,
the men of the Enlightenment valued "religious tolerance, freedom
of expression, reasonableness and moderation, polite learning and
literature, humanitarianism, and cosmopolitanism, virtue and happiness" (Sher 328). All of them considered rhetoric part of their
realm. They wrote and read actively, engaging in an ongoing
conversation about education, politics, and religion through the
many periodicals of the time. The intellectual leaders of the eighteenth century were closely connected with the universities; the

Enlightenment was "in a real sense . . . a University movement" (Sloan 15).

Sher speaks of the "impressive array of literati born between 1710 and the mid or late 1720's," including, among others, Thomas Reid, David Hume, Hugh Blair, George Campbell, William Robertson, Adam Smith, and Alexander Gerard. He points out that these men were born at roughly the same time as Denis Diderot, Immanuel Kant, Thomas Jefferson, and Johann Goethe (8). David Hume published *A Treatise of Human Nature* in 1739–40, the final and fullest statement of the empiricist philosophy of Francis Bacon, John Locke, and George Berkeley. Thomas Reid was the librarian at Marischal College in Aberdeen and later succeeded Adam Smith as professor of moral philosophy at the University of Glasgow. He published his important *Inquiry into the Human Mind on the Principles of Common Sense* in 1764 as an answer to the skepticism of the empiricists Locke and Hume. Reid is generally considered the founder of and spokesperson for the Scottish school of philosophy, which changed the character of nineteenth-century rhetoric, giving it a new terminology and influencing its future direction. Hugh Blair was the minister of St. Giles, and when Adam Smith left Edinburgh to take a position at the University of Glasgow, Blair took over Smith's lecture series in the town. He was subsequently appointed professor of rhetoric at the university, and his lectures had hundreds of editions during the next century in dozens of languages. Adam Smith is best known for his *Inquiry into the Nature and Causes of the Wealth of Nations*, published in London in 1776, but he is known to scholars of rhetoric for his lectures on belles lettres delivered in Edinburgh and his course in rhetoric at the University of Glasgow. William Robertson, one of the leaders of the moderate literati active in the presbytery sessions, was the principal of the University of Edinburgh. Alexander Gerard published his important *Essay on Taste* in 1759.

All of these men were friends and colleagues and met often to exchange ideas. From their positions of power in the church and at the universities, they felt impelled to teach morals, taste, and social responsibility in cultural, political, and artistic matters not only to their students but to their political and religious leaders as well. They were a powerful influence in Edinburgh, in Scotland, in England, on the Continent, and in America.[2] No discussion of eighteenth- and nineteenth-century rhetoric would be understandable without an examination of the Scottish school of philosophy, which so powerfully determined the direction of that study and, in turn, determined the direction of the rhetoric/composition courses in the American universities in the twentieth century.

The Scottish Philosophy of Common Sense

In a memorable quote, George Elder Davie, an eminent Scottish scholar, describes the Scottish Enlightenment as characterized by the philosophers' "success in assimilating and developing the brilliant ideas which had first come to light among the English (in a fit of absence of mind) during the days of Locke and Newton only to be neglected in the era of Walpole" (*Scottish Enlightenment* 7). The "brilliant ideas" to which Davie refers are the treatises of the empiricists, best articulated by Locke in *An Essay Concerning Human Understanding*, published in England in 1690. The assimilation that he refers to is by the Scottish philosopher David Hume in *A Treatise on Human Nature*, published fifty years later, in which he presented the most cogent and complete assimilation of empiricism. The development comes in reaction to empirical skepticism in the new doctrines presented by the Scottish commonsense school.

The philosophical doctrine of empiricism denied the viability of innate ideas and stressed that all ideas came ultimately from sensory perceptions. It denied a priori truth and stressed truth based solely on observation through the senses. It was the outcome of Descartes' tabula rasa and an extension of Bacon's scientific inductive method. The scientific method was well established by the discoveries of Sir Isaac Newton and the founding of the Royal Society of London, but Aristotelian doctrines survived in philosophy and rhetoric until the Scottish philosophers articulated the philosophy of common sense.

James McCosh gives credit for the founding of the Scottish school to Lord Shaftesbury, who, in a series of monographs and articles published between 1707 and 1712, articulated the roots of the Scottish philosophy and introduced the term *sensus communis*, which identified it.

27

Some moral and philosophical truths there are withal so evident in themselves, that it would be easier to imagine half mankind to have run mad, and joined precisely in one and the same species of folly, than to admit any thing as truth which should be advanced against such *natural knowledge, fundamental reason,* and *common sense.* (31)

Most scholars, following the ideas of William Hamilton, professor of logic and metaphysics at Edinburgh (1836–56) and later professor of moral philosophy at Glasgow, see Francis Hutcheson (1694–1746) as the founder of the school. McCosh, however, argues that Hutcheson "did little more than expound these views with less versatility, but in a more equable, thorough, and systematic manner" (35). Hutcheson is best known for his idea of a "moral sense," an innate quality of the human soul that dictates moral decisions, thus departing from Locke and Hume. His monographs, particularly his *Disquisitions on Taste,* set the aesthetic that dominated Scottish thinking during the next two centuries and set the tone for the evolution of criticism as an outgrowth of rhetoric in the nineteenth century.

Though not the founder, Thomas Reid is the scholar most closely associated with the commonsense philosophy. He published his *Inquiry into the Human Mind on the Principles of Common Sense* in 1764 in answer to Locke and Hume, who asserted that objects exist only as images in the mind. In answer Reid said,

If I may trust the faculties that God has given me, I do perceive matter objectively—that is, something which is extended and solid, which may be measured and weighed, is the immediate object of my touch and sight. And this object I take to be matter, and not an idea. And though I have been taught by philosophers, that what I immediately touch is an idea, and not matter; yet I have never been able to discover this by the most accurate attention to my own perceptions. (Qtd. in Davidson 78)

In this treatise, he distinguishes sensation, remembrance, and imagination in connection with an object. Sensation is the knowledge of an object through sensory perception; remembrance is the knowledge of the past existence of an object; imagination is the simple understanding of the existence of an object. Reid argued, "Let scholastic sophisters intangle themselves in their own cobwebs; I am resolved to take my own existence, and the existence of other things, upon trust: and to believe that snow is cold, and honey sweet, whatever they may say to the contrary" (21). Essay 7, from *The Essays on the Intellectual Powers of Man* published in 1785, contains his lectures delivered when he was a regent at King's College, Aberdeen, and professor of moral philosophy at Glasgow. "Of Taste" is one of the first full treatments of this subject, and Reid's doctrine follows his other ideas in that he finds taste to be an innate sensibility. Under this sensibility, he discusses at some length the qualities of novelty, grandeur, and beauty.

Reid, in 1758, formed the Aberdeen Philosophical Society with a group of his friends and colleagues for "the furtherance of thinking and the discussion of philosophical problems." The society's goal is stated in the minutes of the first meeting in what is presumed to be Reid's handwriting.

> The subject of the Discourses and Questions shall be Philosophical, all Grammatical, Historical, and Philolological [sic] Discussions being conceived to be foreign to the Design of the Society. And Philosophical Matters are understood to comprehend, Every Principle of Science which may be deduced by Just and Lawfull Induction from the Phaenomena either of the Human Mind or of the material World. (Qtd. in Davidson 80)

George Campbell was an active member of the society, and his *Philosophy of Rhetoric* was one of the contributions that came out of this remarkable gathering.

Not only Campbell but many other professors of mental and moral philosophy, of logic and metaphysics, of rhetoric and belles lettres used and enlarged the ideas of Reid, as they adapted them to their own disciplines, among them, Adam Smith. After the success of Smith's lectures on rhetoric and belles lettres in Edinburgh, he was invited to Glasgow in 1751 to be professor of logic and in 1752, professor of moral philosophy. His lectures on rhetoric survive in only one set of notes, taken by two students, now reproduced in two modern editions, edited with introductions by John M. Lothian in 1971 and by J. C. Bryce in 1985.

The person who did more than any other to spread the Scottish philosophy was Dugald Stewart, who studied under Reid at Glasgow. Like Reid, his early interest was in mathematics, and under Reid's influence he changed his direction. Stewart owed his interest in philosophy to Reid, but Reid, in turn, owed much to his pupil, who "finished and adorned the work of his master, and by his classical taste has recommended the common-sense philosophy to many who would have turned away with disdain from the simpler manner of Reid" (McCosh 300). Sir William Hamilton, professor of logic and metaphysics at Edinburgh (1836–56), edited the collected works of Reid, a task that was completed by John Veitch, a nineteenth-century professor of logic and rhetoric at Glasgow. Reid was fortunate in the men who followed in his footsteps.

The concept of *taste* (a word translated from the French *goût*), which plays such a major role in the rhetorics of George Campbell and Hugh Blair, was a direct outgrowth of the Scottish philosophy. It was first introduced by Lord Shaftesbury, who avowed that human beings have "a sense of order and proportion" about what they perceive. "Such is a tree with all its branches, an animal with all its members, an edifice with all exterior and interior ornaments" (qtd. in McCosh 35). All of the Scottish philosophers, like Reid, considered taste an inborn quality that could and should be cultivated and that was necessary for the advancement of society. Beauty and good were often equated as linked virtues of human beings and of society.

To promote this idea in their country, the Edinburgh Society for the Encouragement of Arts, Sciences, Manufactures, and Agriculture offered a premium for the best essay on "taste." It was the classical essay of Alexander Gerard, a member of the Aberdeen Philosophical Society, that won the prize (McCosh 191).

In summation, the Scottish commonsense philosophy proceeded on the premise that the human mind could be studied by observation—a tenet that was the beginning of the development of psychology as an academic subject that took place at Aberdeen under the aegis of Alexander Bain in the nineteenth century. From the observation of consciousness, we can know our perceptions and feelings not only through our own experience but also through the experience of others, experience that is communicated to us through language. Thus, language study becomes important in the universities, as professors of rhetoric turn to the insights of literature. Finally, there are innate principles that are prior to and independent of experience. One of these is taste, the sense of beauty common to all human beings, which although innate is capable of development through education. These principles formed the basis for the philosophic education of the eighteenth- and nineteenth-century Scottish universities and greatly influenced instruction in logic, philosophy, belles lettres, and rhetoric.

3

Eighteenth- and Nineteenth-Century Schools and Universities: Rhetoric and Composition

The eighteenth century was a period of upward mobility. With economic stability established, the large and powerful merchant class and those aspiring to better themselves saw that education and language could help them move up. In response, the schoolteachers and grammarians set out to standardize the language.

During this period, there was also a rise in nationalism, which resulted in a new reverence for the English language and for literature. Although men and women of culture read their own vernacular literature, it was still considered folk literature and therefore improper for university instruction. Lectures, coffeehouses, and journals proliferated, however, providing an active forum for such interests. The literary scene in Edinburgh was intellectually lively, and out of this milieu came the popular literary journals like the *Edinburgh Review*, which appeared with its blue and yellow cover in October 1802. None of the writers "engaged in profound investigations," but they wrote "quickly, easily, clearly, pungently, with quite as much information as their readers wished. . . . and were ever in favor of good taste and good sense" (McCosh 340). This journal and others like it served both to standardize and to valorize English. In the middle of the century, the lectures of Adam Smith and Hugh Blair were first delivered in Edinburgh and were well attended by the local populace. When lectures in English literature were brought into the universities in the nineteenth century, the lectures were still marked by a strong sense of nationalism coupled with a strong moral flavor.

Instructors of the eighteenth century felt that in teaching literature they were teaching a vision of the good—an idea that lingered on in academia well into the twentieth century. Since most of the teachers in the eighteenth century were preachers and most university students were training for the ministry, education was understandably closely connected with religion. Religion was considered the rationale for and basis of education and education the route to virtue. Religion and politics both played important parts in the drama of education in the eighteenth century, and the two were never separate after the Jacobitian defeat in 1746.

This fact had been emphasized in the 1707 Act of Union, which, while uniting the parliaments of Scotland and England, allowed Scotland to retain its independence in education and religion. Its universities were well established and highly respected on the Continent and in England. When the 1662 Act of Uniformity was passed, under which all teachers and students were required to swear allegiance to the Church of England, Scottish schools and universities were exempted. Consequently, students who did not wish to take the oath flocked to the Scottish universities or to the Continent, where there were no religious constraints. By the eighteenth century, the dissenting academies, which provided a university-equivalent education, were numerous, while at the same time Oxford and Cambridge had become decadent both morally and educationally. As a result, the academies drew Anglican students as well as dissenters. It is in these academies and in the Scottish universities that innovations took place, that English as an academic subject flourished: instruction in rhetoric and writing came to mean writing English instead of writing Latin.

The Linguistic Situation

In addition to the strong religious and political forces, there were three factors in the linguistic situation of the eighteenth and nineteenth centuries that altered the teaching of rhetoric. The first was the gradual abandonment of Latin as the language of education and culture; the second was the shift from an oral culture to a basically literate culture, from emphasis on speaking to an emphasis on writing; and the third was the proliferation of books and periodicals.

Cultured persons in the eighteenth century read and wrote in Latin. In their grammar schools, they had learned grammar and had written extensively—in Latin. Their religious exercises were in Latin, and they sang psalms in the classical languages. At many schools, all discussion was in Latin except in family groups (McLachlan 34). Literacy was defined as the ability to read and write Latin. It was during this period, however, that objections to such practices were heard as education began to have a more utilitarian end for merchants and men of business. Although the change was gradual, it was during the eighteenth and nineteenth centuries that the shift to English began in the schools and universities.

Another important pedagogical shift that began in the eighteenth century and continued through the nineteenth was the shift from the spoken to the written, the oral to the literate. Rhetoric had been the study of oratory, and university examinations had been oral until almost the middle of the eighteenth century. Until well into the nineteenth century, most important exams remained oral, as the doctoral dissertation defense is today.

Rhetoric had been primarily confined to letter writing and sermons prior to the eighteenth century. As peoples' interests were increasingly served by government representatives and the legal profession during the eighteenth century, oratory became less important, and writing increasingly became the medium of communication and record. Rhetoric traditionally associated with oratory lost favor as a school subject, leaving elocution, a truncated rhetoric dealing only with stylized delivery, as its unsavory residue. Wilbur Samuel Howell, in his discussion of elocution, emphasizes its reductive nature during the two centuries by contrasting the opening line of an elocutionary manual, "Always breathe through the nostrils," and that of Aristotle's *Rhetoric*, "Rhetoric is the counterpart of dialectic" (Howell 145–256).

Another factor in the linguistic situation in this period was the great increase in the reading public, which, in turn, produced a large class of writers who wrote specifically for that public. At the same time that English was making its way into the classroom at all levels, a spirited exchange in writing ensued in the numerous printed publications of the period: books, pamphlets, and periodicals.

Writing manuals and textbooks became more and more numerous to serve this reading and writing public. In the last part of the seventeenth century and the first part of the eighteenth, textbooks and manuals were still largely in Latin. As the lectures changed to English, more and more textbooks in the native tongue were introduced. At first, English and Latin texts were used side by side, since good English textbooks were not available. At some of the schools, Latin textbooks "were abridged and translated by students before being used by them" (McLachlan 22). Instructors often wrote their own; more often, though, dictated lectures became the textbooks for the course.

Schools and Universities

The aim of the eighteenth-century schools was to turn out students who could read and write Latin, so the students embarked on an intensive course of Latin grammar. This endeavor occupied them in the early years. They then studied Greek and rhetoric while continuing to improve their proficiency in Latin by writing Latin verses. Allowance was always made for the young lad o' parts.

The central government began to intervene by imposing a standard on preparatory schools by 1830, but the standard was based on English models. The widespread assumption in the south was that elementary schools provided elementary instruction for the poor students who were not going on to higher education. The English upper classes provided tutors for their children or sent them to grammar schools to prepare for the university. On the other hand, the Scottish public schools, including both parish and burgh schools, drew from a wider social spectrum in preparing students for the university (Myers 81).

By the eighteenth century, Oxford and Cambridge had degenerated into a "preserve for the idle and the rich" (Barnard 24). They were expensive: the annual cost for an undergraduate in the

1830s was between two and three hundred pounds. They were also elitist: undergraduates of noble birth were carefully distinguished from the poorer students by their embroidered gowns of purple silk and a college cap with a gold tassel. In addition, such students were excused from all exams that led to a degree (even though the standards of the tests were low) and were only required to be in residence for thirteen weeks out of the year.

Nicholas Hans in his statistical study of eighteenth-century education points out that "all the leading men of the eighteenth century—Bentham, Butler, Gibbon, Adam Smith, Vicemust [sic] Knox and many lesser lights—condemned the two Universities from their personal experience as students" (42).[1] Vicesimus Knox, headmaster of Tonbridge School from 1778 to 1812, called the requirements for the Oxford degree a "set of childish and useless exercises," which "raise no emulation, confer no honour and promote no improvement." He described the fellows as persons "who neither study themselves nor concern themselves in superintending the studies of others" (qtd. in Barnard 25–26). R. L. Archer, a twentieth-century scholar, describes eighteenth-century Oxford as "a university in which professors had ceased to lecture, and where work was the last thing expected." These students "entered the University not to feed on solid intellectual food, but to enjoy a costly luxury." Oxford at the time was marked by "extravagance, debt, drunkenness, gambling, and an absurd attention to dress" (7). Cambridge did not fare quite as badly as Oxford; but during the eighteenth century, the southern universities were the preserves of a traditional and increasingly decadent cultural elite.

In the late eighteenth century, Oxford and Cambridge offered little that was new for students who came well prepared. Class attendance was low. At Oxford in 1850, "out of 1500 or 1600 undergraduates, the average annual attendance at the modern history course was 8; at botany 6 and at Arabic, Anglo-Saxon, Sanskrit and medicine, none" (Barnard 82). Lectures were dubbed " 'wall lectures' because the lecturers had no other audience than the walls" (Archer 9).

Reform came slowly to Oxford and Cambridge in the middle of the nineteenth century under the Oxford University Act and the Cambridge Reforms of 1854–56. The Founder's Kin scholarships were opened to competition; and for the first time, university business could be carried on in English instead of in Latin (Barnard 123). Life fellowships were abolished, and celibacy was no longer required for the college fellows. In 1871, religious tests for the degree were finally abolished. New professorships were established, the curriculum was broadened, and examinations were made more stringent. In spite of these nineteenth-century reforms, Oxford and Cambridge continued to be aristocratic and extremely conservative throughout the period. Students often preferred the Scottish universities or the dissenting academies, and it is in these institutions that change came about in the way of curricular reforms and innovations. The University of Edinburgh's well-known medical school attracted students from America, as well as from Britain and the Continent.

The Scottish universities offered a general philosophical education under regents and professors. After regenting was abolished, and even after the establishment of a number of professorships, regenting persisted, and the holders of these chairs moved quite easily from one course to another, often presenting the same set of lectures. After 1760, "good theologians and classical scholars were appointed to scientific chairs as a means of reward," and often professors "shifted from one chair to another on seniority rather than qualifications" (Hans 52). The sinecure appointments were held for life, and housing was furnished. The students did not seem to suffer, however, since ordinarily such professors had quite able assistant lecturers who conducted their classes, lectured for them, and customarily took over their chairs at their death.

During the 1700s and the 1800s, the Scottish universities were distinguished by able professors who greatly influenced the direction of English studies in both Britain and America in the nineteenth and twentieth centuries. Such men wrote widely themselves in the journals of the day, were innovators in other fields besides philosophy and rhetoric, and were deeply concerned about questions of morality and politics. Their textbooks, often in the form of published lectures, were widely used on both sides of the Atlantic. The importance of Campbell and Blair and their widespread influence has been well documented, but even this cursory account of eighteenth-century rhetoric would be incomplete without more than a mention of them.[2]

James L. Golden and Edward P. J. Corbett consider Hugh Blair and George Campbell, together with Richard Whately, to be "the great triumvirate of British rhetoricians who came at the end of a long tradition of rhetoric that had its beginning in fifth-century Greece" (1). These authors, however, do not see them as ending the old tradition of rhetoric as much as initiating the new. Blair was born at the beginning of the eighteenth century and died at the end, while Campbell was born one year later and died four years sooner than Blair. Both were ministers and were trained at the universities where they later taught. Campbell attended King's and Marischal Colleges, Blair the University of Edinburgh. Campbell was a member of the Aberdeen Philosophical Society, and Blair was an active member of the moderate literati of Edinburgh. Both were heavily influenced by Thomas Reid and the common-sense philosophers in their conceptions of rhetoric, and both produced books that were widely influential in rhetoric in the British and American universities.

Hugh Blair was born in Edinburgh, where he lived all his life. He studied under John Stevenson, a professor of logic, who was one of the earliest professors to include English literature in his course. Stevenson taught standards of taste and criticism in his classes and also taught his students how to speak and write the London standard. Stevenson used Locke's logic to demonstrate that knowledge comes from sensory experience. The rules of what Stevenson called this "natural logic" were the rules of induction (Emerson 468). Under Stevenson's direction, Blair wrote and publicly read an essay, "On the Beautiful," which may have influenced his later thinking and writing. He was appointed to a pastorate in Fife, to the Canongate Church in Edinburgh, and then to the church of St. Giles, where he remained until his retirement. When Adam Smith left Edinburgh, Hugh Blair took over his highly successful lectures.[3] Because of the like success of his lectures, he was appointed to the Regius Professorship of Rhetoric and Belles Lettres in 1762. Blair indicated his aim in the first lecture. "Whether the influence of the speaker, or the entertainment of the hearer, be consulted; whether utility or pleasure be the principal aim in view, we are prompted, by the strongest motives, to study how we may communicate our thoughts to one another with most advantage" (Lecture 1). Later in the same lecture, he spoke directly to his own audience: "The study of composition, important in itself at all times, has acquired additional importance from the taste and manners of the present age." The word *taste* recurs again and again, and the concept is taken up in some detail in the second lecture. He defines taste as "the power of receiving pleasure from the beauties of nature and of art," and he demonstrates his connection with the commonsense philosophers when he explains that it is a "power or faculty in the human mind . . . an internal sense of beauty, which is natural to men, and which, in its application to particular objects, is capable of being guided and enlightened by reason" (Lecture 1). Blair, under the influence of Stevenson and Smith, was able to articulate and disseminate the rhetoric that arose out of empiricism and the Scottish philosophy.

"Blair was said to have been born with a clerical spoon in his mouth" (Meikle 91). His career seemed to follow an unbroken path to success, in spite of a personality marked by vanity, dullness, and a marked ineptitude for public speaking. One of the stories told of him was that he kept a mirror on the floor of his church, so that he could be sure that the flow of his cassock was in order (Meikle 92). In spite of these foibles, Blair had an immense reputation in his time. No one was more respected, and his lectures, which he read unchanged for twenty-four years, were successful because they spoke to the needs of the time. Their spirit reflected the interest in English literature that derived from the new nationalism and the new philosophy. These lectures demonstrate the beginning of the shift from rhetoric to criticism. "Rhetoric is not so much a practical art," Blair asserts, "as a speculative science; and the same instructions which assist others in composing will assist them in judging of, and relishing, the beauties of composition" (Blair, Lecture 1, 8). Blair's lectures filled the gap left by the old rhetoric and logic, which no longer seemed relevant.

> As rhetoric has been sometimes thought to signify nothing more than the scholastic study of words, and phrases, and tropes, so criticism has been considered as merely the art of finding faults; as the frigid application of certain technical terms, by means of which persons are taught to cavil and censure in a learned manner. But this is the criti-

cism of pedants only. True criticism is a liberal and hu-
mane art. It is the offspring of good sense and refined
taste. (Blair, Lecture 1)

The *Lectures* were published in 1783 and, in the following eighteen
years, were translated into German, French, Spanish, and Italian,
and were adapted into the Russian in 1837. Robert Schmitz lists
twenty-six editions in Great Britain, thirty-seven in the United
States, and fifty-two abridged editions.

Campbell, like Blair, was the minister of one of the Aberdeen
city churches and a professor and later principal of Marischal
College. He first gained recognition for his *Dissertation on Miracles*,
an answer to one aspect of Hume's religious skepticism. One of
his fellow professors remarked to his class in church history that
"Hume's attack on miracles laid the theologians flat on their backs,
and they did not regain their erect position till Campbell came and
set them up again" (P. J. Anderson, *Studies* 82). His *Philosophy of
Rhetoric* was written while he attended the meetings of the Aberdeen Philosophical Society, and he read and received suggestions
from that group. It bears the strong marks of Thomas Reid and the
commonsense school of philosophy and psychology. In chapter 1,
he defines the "ends of speaking" as reducible to four: "every
speech being intended to enlighten the understanding, to please
the imagination, to move the passions, or to influence the will"
(Golden and Corbett 145).

Campbell is probably most famous for his attack on the
syllogism in which he argues that it proves its conclusion by citing
as evidence the same point stated in a more general way in its
premise. He states that this is "a *begging of the question* and is . . .
the proving of a thing by itself, whether expressed in the same or
in different words" (173–74). In his attack on the syllogism, he
was attacking the base and foundation of traditional logic. In
shifting from deduction in the syllogism to induction and the
scientific method of Bacon and Reid, he was changing the fundamental nature of logic and rhetoric.

Pedagogy in Rhetoric and Composition

It is difficult to document the way rhetoric and composition
were actually taught during this period, since much instruction

was oral and since instruction in writing was a part of every course and considered the responsibility of every instructor. Ian Michael, in his study of textbooks of the period, maintains that there is "less textbook evidence for the teaching of composition than for any other aspect of English" (315). Other sources are not much more productive. In this chapter, I have drawn from textbooks, lectures, students' notes of lectures, books on education, and university calendars for the nineteenth century. Such sources are not always reliable because, in many cases, they deal with what individuals felt ought to be done either by themselves or by others and not with what actually took place in the classroom. Because of the wide practice of dictating lectures, students' notes are more reliable than they might appear.

During the eighteenth and nineteenth centuries, the teaching of composition proceeded in a number of different ways and in a number of different courses. Most important, all teachers in the Scottish universities from grammar school onward felt that writing proficiency was their responsibility. Writing assignments and writing instruction were a part of every course. The separate composition course as we know it today had no place in the eighteenth- and nineteenth-century Scottish curriculum.

Medieval pedagogy lasted well into the eighteenth and nineteenth centuries. The trivium of grammar, logic, and rhetoric provided solid training in communication skills during the early part of the eighteenth century. Memorization and modeling were common methods of improving students' writing, and instructors believed that to learn to read one had first to learn to spell and that the study of grammar was basic to writing instruction. But the grammar was the grammar of Latin since writing instruction was writing Latin. Throughout the period and well into the twentieth century, grammar and writing instruction were closely connected. As part of their instruction in Latin, however, students had been required to translate "into a good English stile" (Michael 274); and as late as the end of the nineteenth century, proficiency in English was still tested by translation from Latin. Whether it was in Latin or English or in Latin *and* English, exercises in grammar and translation were an integral part of writing instruction. A master at Eton shared the common view that the only way to improve a student's English was through translation, but, in

41

1867, he urged that French or another modern language be substituted for Latin (Michael 311). As the study of modern languages came into the curriculum, it was considered a viable method of improving English.

What we would now call basic English was an important part of writing instruction in the Scottish universities. While England's universities were elitist and exclusive, the more democratic Scottish universities during the 1700s and well into the 1800s were dealing with a different student population and therefore saw as an important part of their purview the need to eradicate "provincial accents or phrases." Consequently, elocution gained importance in the curriculum. Again, the main goal of the universities was to train ministers for the church.

Rhetoric took on a new form under the influence of the Scottish commonsense philosophy, and classical rhetoric was often delegated to that part of the course that dealt with oral delivery. Written and oral skills and Latin and English were taught side by side, instruction in one reinforcing instruction in the other. The master often read a letter aloud, and the student then transposed it from Latin to Latin, then translated it from Latin to English, and finally transposed it from English to English (Michael 308). It was not until late in the nineteenth century that oral and written skills were separated into different courses and different departments.

Just as there was a close association between the teaching of Latin and English, between oral and written skills, there was also a close association between reading and writing and between literature and composition. At the Scottish universities, works of literature, both classical and English, were first introduced into the rhetoric course as models for good oratory and writing. Literature was a sort of "window display, to be taken in snippets . . . as illustrations for rhetorical techniques" (McMurtry 122). Literature served rhetoric in a very real way because students were often required to imitate the models. As science took over in the humanities, there was a need for observable physical data. The text became the data, and the text was literature. As the examples were drawn more and more from English literature, interest shifted during the nineteenth century from rhetoric to an emphasis on the literature itself, especially evident in the courses of William

Edmondstoune Aytoun. Whenever rhetoric and literature are taught together, literature wins out with both instructors and students, and the nineteenth century was no exception. Nevertheless, the early professors of literature considered writing instruction their responsibility. Even though English literature came to dominate the newly formed English departments, composition was an important part not only of the literature course but of all courses in the Scottish universities during this period. With its philosophically based curriculum and its need to educate men of the cloth, Scotland saw communication skills, both spoken and written, as central to the entire educational endeavor.

The Lecture System and Writing

During this period, there were important differences between the English tutorial system and the lectures at the Scottish universities. In the Scottish system, the lectures were augmented by the catechetical system, whereby the professor lectured for one hour a day and spent an additional one or two hours questioning the students about the material covered in the lecture and responding to student essays. The lecture system differed from instructor to instructor; McLachlan describes some of the methods:

> Some of the later tutors dictated word for word. Others like Doddridge and Priestley read their lectures and then handed over the MSS. to be copied by their pupils at leisure. Belsham spoke "from brief hints and imperfect notes." Pye Smith provided pupils with an outline of his principal course. Many lectures were printed locally for the use of students, and one course given by Priestley at Hackney College and previously at Warrington was printed "in order to save the students the trouble of transcribing them." (23)

The Scottish universities, like the dissenting academies in England and in contrast to the English universities, had a tradition of free discussion.

After the medieval fashion, students often used their class notes as their text. Textbooks were expensive and students were

43

often poor. The eighteenth century's published lectures by Blair and Campbell served as textbooks for almost a hundred years in the United States—one of the important ways that Scottish education influenced American education. Few of the dissenting academies had libraries, and students who often could not afford texts used their professors' personal libraries instead. But, professors in the academies were underpaid, so books of all kinds were scarce.

The custom of dictates provided accurate textbooks for the students, but there were abuses. The students' notes from David Masson's course, for example, do not vary over thirty years by more than an occasional word or two. Robert Schmitz tells the story of students who were following Masson's lecture from sets of previous years' notes. They objected to changes in the lectures, and when Masson deviated from their copies, they would shuffle their feet in protest, whereupon Masson, rising, would remark, "Gentlemen . . . , as I have been in the habit of saying," and would return to his previous years' notes (qtd. in Schmitz 67). J. D. Comrie writes about the lectures delivered by the three Munros—father, son, and grandson—who held the chair of anatomy at the University of Edinburgh for 150 years. The grandson, who held the chair in the nineteenth century, customarily read from his grandfather's lectures written about a century before; and even the shower of peas with which the expectant students greeted his annual reference, "When I was a student at Leyden in 1719," failed to induce him to alter the dates (Comrie 19–27).

As previously stated, some students developed a shorthand for taking notes (EUL Ms. Gen. 49D); others used phonetic spellings (GUL Ms. Gen. 700). Professor George Jardine at Glasgow objected to this procedure because the student "is constantly occupied with the mechanical operation of transferring the words of the lecture into his note-book." Consequently, his mind is not engaged, and "when he leaves college, accordingly, his port-folio, and not his memory, contains the chief part of the instruction which he carries away." He suggested instead that, after leaving the classroom, students immediately review the lecture in their minds and "commit to writing in their own composition, whatever they judge to be of leading importance" (278). In this way, he asserted, "The students have to remember,—to select and arrange

44

the materials furnished to them, and to express, on the spur of the occasion, their ideas in plain and perspicuous language" (289). This appears, in fact, to be the manner in which the two students mentioned earlier collaborated in taking Adam Smith's lecture notes (Bryce 4). Students often embellished their notes with drawings and bits of humor; one set contains scenes from Glasgow in the margins and a reference to Aristotle as the "Rev. J. G. Aristotle" (GUL BC 28-H.3). In a moral philosophy course, one student complained that the professor was dictating "fast enough in all conscience to keep 20 persons writing" and that he did not "feel very morally philosophical" (EUL Ms. Gen. 850).

The reader of these notes is inclined to feel sympathy for these students, but the value in ridding students of their Scottish rusticims and in training them in the mechanics of a written standard cannot be overestimated, and certainly Jardine's suggestion of summarizing the lectures in a written composition proved an invaluable and productive exercise in selecting and organizing a body of information. These lectures with their various systems of notetaking were obviously used to supplement textbooks and instruction in writing.

In addition to their notetaking, whatever form it might have taken, Scottish university students often continued with their preparatory school exercises, inherited from the medieval universities and the Latin tradition. While the English universities restricted higher education to a small percentage of the population, Scotland still opened its doors to all able students who sought an education. Consequently, university courses were designed to supplement their preparatory training and to fill in deficiencies.

Grammar and Writing

Grammar was stressed at all levels, and it was considered a necessary part of instruction in both Latin and English composition. Based on the assumption that there was a universal grammar common to all languages, the Latin system was adapted without change to English. In the grammar schools, the students were often expected to know their grammar books by heart. Memorization of books and literary passages was a common practice, even at the university level, since students were expected to have patterns of good writing in their heads. In addition, parsing and the correction of "false English" were widely used. Students were expected to correct sentences that had errors of spelling, syntax, or punctuation and to give the rule that had been broken. The master then corrected the exercises orally and returned them to the students who, with the help of their classmates, made their own corrections in writing. Because paper was expensive, students often wrote their first version on a slate and then copied the corrected version into their notebooks (Michael 327).

Grammar exercises associated with the old rhetoric were widely used by students at all levels: imitation; varying, which involved changing a sentence into all of its possible forms; paraphrasing; and prosing, turning verse into prose. Transposition, a common exercise, was "the placing of Words out of their natural Order, to render the Sound of them more agreeable to the Ear" (qtd. in Michael 283). Elliptical exercises were sentences with omitted words, which the student was expected to supply. Many of these exercises, closely associated with the old rhetoric, began to die out by the nineteenth century, but translation, from Latin to English and later from a modern foreign language, continued to be used well into the twentieth century.

Examinations and Themes

The catechetical system, whereby students were quizzed on the material in the lecture, was initially largely oral. Toward the middle of the nineteenth century, the written examination began to replace the oral question-and-answer format. In the description of his course on moral philosophy, a professor at the University of Edinburgh asserted that class time was to be devoted "partly to examinations, written and oral." He added that "subjects are also prescribed for elaborate Essays, as well as for briefer occasional exercises" (EUL Calendar 1859–60). In the same calendar, Alexander Campbell Fraser, professor of logic and metaphysics, wrote that class hours are devoted to lectures and "also to a Discipline, by means of Conversations, short Exercises, and Essays, meant to train the members to logical habits and a reflective life. General Examinations, at which answers are returned in writing to questions proposed by the Professor, are held at intervals in the course of the Session."

In general, the practice of writing instruction followed the recommendation of the 1831 report by the Royal Commissioners: "In addition to Examinations, Exercises and Essays should be required from all the regular Students in each class, and ought to be criticized by the professor" (*Report*, 1831, 35). Consequently, instruction in writing was never confined to any single course.

Professor Robert Eden Scott, in giving evidence before that commission in 1827, described the manner in which he conducted his class in moral philosophy, which met for two and a half hours during the day. The first half hour was spent in oral examination of the preceding day's lecture, "with the students reading aloud their written answers to questions assigned the day before." A considerable part of the afternoon hour was spent "in the practice of composition," and subjects were prescribed "and a time fixed, before which the essays must be left by the authors at the Professor's house" (*Royal Commissioners* 40).

George Jardine at Glasgow also had a procedure for assigning themes. In his 1825 *Outlines of a Philosophical Education*, he stated that themes should be "prescribed frequently and regularly" and that the subjects should be "numerous and various." In his work, he also outlined a four-ordered sequence for his assignments, calling for escalating study, proof, argument, and understanding (291–360).

Responses to Writing

The University of Edinburgh Library has in its manuscript library a collection of twelve essays written by John Dick Peddies in 1844–45 for William Spalding's course in rhetoric and belles lettres (EUL Ms. Gen. 769D). Written during Peddies' last year at the university, these themes vary in length from twelve to forty-two pages, covering such subjects as "Remarks on Harris' Treatise on Music, Painting, and Poetry" and "Remarks on Different Points in the Association Theory of Beauty." Professor Spaldings' comments are not lengthy and are generally complimentary, and it may be assumed that they were augmented by oral comments. He corrects many of the same kinds of errors that twentieth-century students make. In notes from David Masson's class in 1881–82, the student jots down the professor's assignment and instructions on the last page of volume 4: "Attend to neatness of form, expression and pointing, as well as the matter" (EUL Ms. DK. 4.28–30).

Throughout the eighteenth and nineteenth centuries, with few exceptions, responding to students' writing was a matter of correction rather than of appraisal, and more often than not it was oral. Students often read their work aloud, and it was criticized publicly by the professor or by their classmates or by both. In the lower schools, it was largely correction of mechanical errors. Ian Michael describes John Walker's "Hints for Correcting and Improving Juvenile Composition":

> The pupil writes a first draft on loose paper. Next day he copies it, with amendments, onto the lefthand page of an exercise book. He reads the theme, without interruption, to the teacher, who then takes it sentence by sentence and shows the pupil "where he has erred, either in the thought, the structure of the sentence, the grammar of it, or the choice of words." (Qtd. in Michael 222)

The pupil then makes a fair copy on the right-hand page of his exercise book (Michael 315). Michael comments that Walker "understandably advises that classes for composition should be as small as possible" (315).

Professor Jardine's method of responding to themes, outlined in a chapter titled "On the Method of Determining the Merits of the Themes," sounds remarkably modern. Faced with a class of nearly two hundred students, he contends that "experience and habit enable the teacher to execute this work more expeditiously than might at first sight be believed" (364). He urges that "the professor must touch their [students'] failings with a gentle hand" (365). He further suggests for large classes the use of "examinators," ten or twelve students from the class who read other students' written work, with the professor selecting works that "abound with defects" for his own inspection, which he returns with remarks "most likely to encourage, and to direct future efforts" (371).

The Scottish universities served a special purpose and fulfilled the special needs of their people. They took their students where they found them and gave them a general philosophic education. But during the eighteenth and early nineteenth centuries, the system was coming under increasing attack.

The Nineteenth-Century Reforms

The Scottish universities did not have entrance exams before 1889, and students continued to arrive at the universities at an early age. (Thomas Reid, for example, entered Marischal College when he was twelve years old [McCosh 195].) In general, students went to the universities when they had exhausted the education that was available to them in their parish or burgh schools. The age at which they matriculated depended on the preparatory education that was available to them and on their own ability. This system grew out of the democratic ideal that saw education as a necessity for an informed citizenry and as the right of every male citizen.[4] It was the precursor for specialized study and provided a broad philosophical education for a great number of students.

Increasingly after the 1707 Act of Union, the Scottish universities came under attack. During the 1700s, when the English and European universities were in decline, the Scottish universities thrived. They were highly innovative and pioneered in studies that are now familiar in contemporary curricula. Newton's theories were first taught at the northern universities, and German philosophy, economics, and agriculture were a regular part of the curriculum. Medicine, as an academic discipline, was introduced first in the Scottish universities. But in the nineteenth century, Scottish education was accused of being too elementary. Dr. Samuel Johnson, never an admirer of the Scots, criticized their universities for being superficial. Francis Jeffrey, in turn, defended the Scottish system:

> I endorse, on the whole the justice of the reproach that has been levelled against our general national instruction—that our knowledge, though more general, is more superficial than with our neighbors. That is quite true, and our system leads to it, but I think it is a great good

on the whole, because it enables relatively large numbers of people to get—not indeed profound learning, for that is not to be spoken of—but that knowledge which tends to liberalize and make intelligent the mass of our population. (*Evidence, Edinburgh* 389)

The reformers criticized the practical education that emphasized composition. A professor from Glasgow asserted in his statement to the university commission,

With regard to the classes of Logic and Moral Philosophy—they are both to be considered in their practical tendency classes for teaching composition—but these exercises in composition are too frequent and too long. . . . The mere exercise of composition is esteemed far more important than any preparation for it. . . . Essays of a prodigious length are given in Logic, and [students] are not able to give sufficient attention to the cultivation of taste according to the pure models and critical principles of Greece. (Qtd. in Davie, *Democratic Intellect* 28)

The English and even some Scots, mostly the upper class, saw reform as conformity to the English system and a positive move. There were, however, basic philosophic differences. As Lyon Playfair put it, "The English Universities . . . teach men how to spend 1,000 pounds a year with dignity and intelligence while the Scotch Universities teach them how to make 1,000 pounds a year with dignity and intelligence" (qtd. in R. D. Anderson, *Education* 35–36). In England, education was open only to the few, while the Scottish idea was to provide a broad and general education for the many. During the nineteenth century, however, the Scottish universities, through a series of "reforms" lost their special character and became, in effect, English. The institution of entrance exams in 1889 resulted in closing the door to all but the most able and best prepared students.

But there were general problems with the Scottish system, as well as problems with the individual institutions. Oxford and Cambridge had always had live-in students and tended to exercise control in matters of morals and behavior. They were in effect "schools of manners" (R. D. Anderson, *Education* 35). The Scottish students, on the other hand, lived in lodgings and often brought their own food with them from their rural homes. As a result, there was little collegiate life. Since the professors were supported by fees, anyone from the town who paid the appropriate price could attend the lectures, which, as a result, tended to be large, public performances directed to anonymous audiences. Also, the professorships became, in some cases, sinecures, which were held for life, long after the professor could perform his duties, in which case he hired an assistant to read his lectures. The biggest perceived problem was, of course, the lack of the entrance exam, which, although it ensured open access, also forced the universities to lower their standards. This is an all too familiar story for twentieth-century American institutions after open admissions were instituted in the twentieth century.

In addition to the general problems of the Scottish system, the individual institutions each had special problems, as control shifted in the eighteenth century from the church to the state. At Edinburgh, the town council controlled the university and did not take kindly to parliamentary suggestions. At Aberdeen, where two colleges existed side by side, one serving the city students, the other the more rural population, they felt the need to combine the schools to prevent duplication. St. Andrews was small and poor. It possessed a chair of medicine but no medical school, and to relieve their poverty, St. Andrews sold medical degrees, a practice that was reformed but not ended in 1826 (R. D. Anderson, *Education* 39). Glasgow was in the midst of an internal dispute over the refusal by the professors to admit the medical professors to the "faculty," an exclusion that deprived them of certain professorial privileges.

Two Royal Commissions, appointed in 1826 and 1876 to study the universities, were followed in not very rapid succession by parliamentary regulatory acts in 1858 and 1889. These commissions were concerned not only with the administrative and financial matters but also with curriculum and pedagogy. They were followed in 1858 and 1889 by acts of Parliament, which imposed certain regulations. The 1858 act was ignored for the most part, and real changes did not take place until 1889, the most significant of which was the institution of entrance exams.

The report by the Royal Commission of 1826 was greeted with general hostility. Influenced strongly by English and Scottish anglophiles, it emphasized study of the classics and ignored science as a legitimate study. The suggested entrance exam was opposed by the University of Edinburgh, where open lectures were seen as serving the interests of the town and its many part-time and adult students. The Scottish universities felt that they were serving a different clientele than that served by the English universities. R. D. Anderson reports on a questionnaire administered by George Ramsay in 1876 to his junior class in Latin at Glasgow, which met at 8:00 and 11:00 A.M.

Of the 283 students who replied, 97 came only to the 8 o'clock class, and then went on to their work, mostly as "clerks in law offices" (56) or teachers (30). A further 44 came to the 11 o'clock class, but also had full-time jobs. Of the remaining 142 students, 74 were free in the winter but had to work in the summer; they included 17 teachers, mostly from the Highlands, who obtained substitutes during the university session. That left only 60 students who had no other cares. (*Education* 76)

This was even more true of other courses outside of the humanities. At Edinburgh, for example, many of the students in the engineering class "went on to a full day's work as draughtsmen or assistant engineers." The professor of political economy held his class at 5:00 P.M. to accommodate his students, most of whom worked in offices or banks. Consequently, when the Scots instituted entrance exams they were reluctant to exclude these students (R. D. Anderson, *Education* 76–77). A compromise was reached in that the exam should be introduced gradually and only for degree students and not as a requirement for older students.

Aberdeen also opposed any barrier to access and felt that the university's relationship with the parish schools was a "vital national tradition to be maintained at all costs" (R. D. Anderson, *Education* 48). The report of the Royal Commission of 1826 was published during the Reform Bill Crisis, so its results were largely ignored until 1858 when a parliamentary act was passed. This act finally came about because of agitation from within the universities themselves and because of pressure from the new societies of university graduates, which grew up at Aberdeen and Glasgow. The 1858 Regulatory Act stipulated that English literature be added to the logic course with the idea that it eventually be made a separate course, as it was at Edinburgh, and that it be made compulsory. The result was the creation of a chair in English at Glasgow; while at Aberdeen and St. Andrews for thirty years, English literature was taught by the professor of logic (R. D. Anderson, *Education* 72). But by and large, because of general hostility and because of other concerns, little was accomplished by the 1858 act.

The Royal Commission of 1876 issued a report followed by the act of 1889, which put in place a number of reforms that, in effect, made the Scottish universities conform to the English model and that set up policies that are still in effect in the twentieth century. They included the institution of the entrance exam and the setting up of an executive commission that had the power to grant degrees and to institute new degrees. The curricular choices were enlarged, and faculties of science were added in all of the universities.

By the end of the nineteenth century, the Scottish universities had lost their special character and their affinity with the American universities. The effect of the German universities was felt in the United States and Britain as well. This study is, in effect, concerned with the close connection between the Scottish and American universities during the early part of the nineteenth century, with the emerging differences at the end of that century, and, most important, with the effect that such early connections and final differences have had on the direction of twentieth-century American education, in general, and composition and rhetoric, in particular.

4

The University of Edinburgh

Edinburgh was the legal and ecclesiastical capital of Scotland, and its influence in the eighteenth century made it an intellectual and literary center as well. During the first quarter of the nineteenth century, its population almost doubled—from eighty thousand to nearly one hundred fifty thousand (Saunders 81). It drew from a number of small industries, which made it a commercial center second only to Glasgow. People from the surrounding region, who gravitated to Edinburgh either temporarily as travelers or permanently as residents, gave the city a prosperous and busy air in the early part of the nineteenth century. The influx of tourists from England and the Continent gave it a cosmopolitan air. Its imposing architecture lent solidity, and the pattern of elegant living thrived in the city during the first quarter of the new century.

By 1830, however, circumstances were changing. There were the deaths of the interesting older generation, the moderate literati of the Enlightenment. More and more, ambitious young people left for London, taking on the manners and customs of that city and eschewing the old Scottish way of life. In particular, the Scots language was a matter of concern, and it was universally agreed that it should be eradicated. An early law at the University of Edinburgh censored the students for cursing, swearing, or speaking in Scots (Hutton 15), and a number of elocutionists made a good living in the town itself by giving lessons in how to speak the proper London dialect.

But the town continued to thrive. It became a medical center, and doctors and lawyers, instead of divines, dominated city life as Edinburgh took on a civic consciousness. "By 1830 Edinburgh was humming with good causes and transcendental schemes of human progress and perfection" (Saunders 93). There were economic, social, and intellectual expansions as Edinburgh took its place as one of the central cities of Great Britain. Finally, its citizens, before the century was over, began to see themselves as *Britishers* rather than as the narrower *Scots*.

The universities, however, still saw themselves in the old pattern, proud of the educational heritage that had so successfully served their people. They continued to accept students at an early age directly from their parish and burgh schools. It was an ideal system for serving the scattered people of Scotland. The universities offered an arts course—a philosophic general education—which was the prerequisite for the professional specialties. It was very different from English education, but by the end of the century, through a series of so-called reforms, the distinctive pattern of Scottish education would be abandoned as the universities became English. It is this change that this study traces at the University of Edinburgh, at Glasgow, and at the universities of the north—Aberdeen and St. Andrews. The universities in the first part of the nineteenth century were quite different from those of the last twenty years and also different from their English counterparts.

> In English ears, the words, "college days" suggest splen-
> did buildings, luxurious rooms, and rich endowments, as
> the reward of successful industry. In Oxford and in Cam-
> bridge, the students were young men between nineteen
> and twenty-three, who enjoyed themselves in every possi-
> ble social way, and who spent handsome allowances. . . .
> The Universities north of the Tweed . . . in the second
> decade of the nineteenth century, had no prizes to offer,
> no fellowships, no scholar-ships; they had nothing what-
> ever to give but an education, and the teaching of severe
> lessons in the discipline of poverty and self-denial. (Qtd.
> in Hutton 28)

The students at Edinburgh came from the neighboring region, often walking to the university as Thomas Carlyle did.[1] David

Masson, in his *Edinburgh Sketches and Memories*, describes that early walk.

> Early in November 1809 two boys walked together from Ecclefechan in Dumfriesshire to Edinburgh, to attend the classes in the University there. The distance, as the crow flies, is about sixty miles; and the boys took three days to it. The elder, who had been at College in the previous session, and therefore acted as the guide, generally stalked on a few paces ahead, whistling an Irish tune to himself. The younger, who was not quite fourteen years of age, and had never been out of Dumfriesshire before, followed rather wearily, irritated by the eternal Irish tune in front of him, but mainly given up to his own "bits of reflections in the silence of the moors and hills." The elder of the two boys was a Thomas Smail, afterwards of some note as a Burgher minister in Galloway; the younger was Thomas Carlyle. (226)

These boys came to a city that was riddled with crime and infested with disease, particularly in the area where the students lived. There was the risk of walking alone at night that encouraged the students to stay in their lodgings and study rather than venture forth. Unlike the English and American colleges, the University of Edinburgh did not furnish any lodgings for their students. The students found what housing they could within their often meager means. They attended lectures in large classrooms, queued for books at the library, and returned to their lodgings, with small opportunity for making friends. Their lives were, for the most part, lonely and isolated. For food, they usually had what they could prepare themselves often from supplies that they had brought from their homes.

They also brought with them their passion for education. "The Parish teacher prided himself on the number of students he sent to college; their families pinched to keep them there and shone in the reflected glory" (Saunders 309). Furthermore, the emphasis on science and philosophy, the critical mindset of the professors, and their eagerness to explore new avenues of knowledge could not fail to infect the students. This attitude, more than anything else, distinguished the northern universities from those in the south.

The university buildings themselves left much to be desired. The New College was begun in 1793, but construction had been halted by war. The area was littered with building materials, and when construction was resumed, it added to the general confusion. Students wandered in and out of classes, since, again, anyone could attend the lectures who paid the professor's fee and obtained a "class ticket." In 1812, "snowball throwing, 'cutting doors' and writing on walls were nuisances" (qtd. in I. Campbell, "Carlyle" 56). For the Edinburgh student there was no ivory tower.

Two degrees in arts were in existence at this time: the M.A. and the B.A., which was a truncated master's degree. The B.A. was seldom awarded, and the custom of graduating fell into abeyance at the Scottish universities. Between 1788 and 1798, Edinburgh had no graduates; between 1800 and 1810, there were only thirty-one degrees given (Morgan 76–77). In the Royal Commissioners report of 1826, it was determined,

> In general there was either no examination [for gradua-
> tion], or a very slight one, not calculated to ascertain the
> qualifications of the candidate. This mode of bestowing
> Degrees was sufficient to lower them in public estimation.
> They ceased to be objects of solicitude, and in general
> have been viewed with so little respect, that at Edinburgh
> and Glasgow comparatively few individuals have of late
> applied for them. (Morgan 78)

The class tickets, which certified the student's attendance at the lectures, became the "accepted evidence of advanced study" (Saunders 308). What the students did have at Edinburgh was access to a library of seven hundred thousand volumes—albeit for only two hours a day, from 11:00 A.M. to 1:00 P.M. Students were urged to bring with them a "written list of such as they wish in addition to their matriculation ticket and the ticket of some one professor" (Bower 3). The library was something they had not had in their parish schools or in their homes. David Masson's report of Carlyle's description of the library in those days leaves something to be desired.

The students came at definite hours, and ranged themselves in *queue* in some passage, or at some entry, waiting
for the opening of the door, and perhaps battering at it
when the sub-librarian inside was dilatory. He was a sulky
gentleman, of Celtic blood and stout build, who regarded
the readers as his natural enemies; and, when he did open
the door, he generally presented himself in *rear* to the im-
patient crowd, taking care to bend his body at the final
moment so as to administer one last impediment of con-
tempt for the entrants and send some of them sprawling.
That was the kind of encouragement to reading . . . that
he and other University students had in those days. (241)

Nevertheless, Carlyle always maintained that reading had sustained
him and educated him during his university days, and always after
he found that "I could go into the books that treated of these
things, and try anything I wanted to make myself master of gradually, as I found it suit me" (Carlyle).

Religious restrictions, unlike at the English universities, were
nonexistent at Edinburgh, a point that the 1822 *Edinburgh Students' Guide* makes clear.

It may be proper to mention for the information of
strangers, that no oath, nor subscription to any articles of
religion, nor Confession of Faith, are required, as is the
case at the universities of Oxford and Cambridge. Persons
of every profession of religion are freely admitted,
whether Catholics or Protestants, and no questions asked.
(Bower 6)

There were four faculties at the University of Edinburgh in
the early part of the century: literature and philosophy; theology;
law; and medicine. The guide announced that the fee for the class
ticket for rhetoric and belles lettres was four pounds, four shillings,
some one pound more than the Greek, Latin, and math professors
received, two pounds more than the theology professors, but
about the same as the medical and law faculties. The rhetoric class
met at noon on Wednesday, and no one could obtain an M.A.
without it (Bower 25). The purpose of the course as described in

the guide was "to initiate the youth into a knowledge of the principles of criticism, and to form their taste in regard to polite literature" (Bower 25). The guide points out that the Regius Professorship of Rhetoric and Belles Lettres was founded in 1760 with Hugh Blair as its first holder. "Previous to this period no lectures were professedly delivered upon these subjects in the University." The only exception was Dr. Stevenson, the eighteenth-century professor of logic, who considered himself the first professor of belles lettres and English literature (Bower 24).

The University of Edinburgh holds an important place in the history of English language studies because it is at this university that the study of English literature as a legitimate academic subject developed, and it was largely due to its influence and the popularity of the rhetoric professors that this study was instituted as a requirement in the arts programs of all the Scottish universities.[2] The study of belles lettres and English literature was initiated in the university by John Stevenson (1730–75) in his course on logic, metaphysics, and rhetoric. He devoted one hour to rhetoric, in which he read Homer's *Iliad,* Longinus' *On the Sublime,* and Aristotle's *Poetics.* He introduced English literary studies by providing examples from John Dryden, Joseph Addison, Alexander Pope, and other authors from English and French literature (Meikle 90). He always delivered his logic lectures in Latin and his rhetoric lectures in English (Bator 52) and had in one of his classes a student named Hugh Blair.

Between 1748 and 1751, Adam Smith delivered a course of lectures on belles lettres in Edinburgh. As lectures were common in the life of the city and were well attended, and as this was one of the few educational opportunites for women at the time, such town lectures were well attended by both women and men. Henry Home, Lord Kames, seems to have been the guiding force behind these particular lectures. When Adam Smith left to take a post in Glasgow in 1751, Robert Watson took over Smith's popular lecture series until 1756, when he was invited to become professor of logic, rhetoric, and metaphysics at St. Andrews. Three years later, Hugh Blair, who was the minister of the large church of St. Giles, took over the lectures. Blair's lectures were moved in 1762 to the university, and he was appointed professor of rhetoric by the Edinburgh town council with no salary. Shortly after, the

Regius Professorship of Rhetoric and Belles Lettres was established with a salary of seventy pounds a year. Because of his successful lectures and as compensation for being denied the principalship for which he had applied, Blair was invited to occupy it (Horn papers, EUL Ms. Gen. 1824, Box 2). Blair is well known to us through the publication of his lectures, which were widely used in both the British and American universities and for which he received the handsome sum of fifteen hundred pounds. Blair, better known for his writing than for his speaking ability, was the first person to make the connection between rhetoric and criticism, a connection that distinguishes and dominates the lectures of the next century. In the nineteenth century, the chair may have been more distinguished for the people who did not take the chair—Sir Walter Scott and Thomas Carlyle—than for those who applied and were accepted. One outstanding exception is William Edmondstoune Aytoun who held the chair from 1845 to 1865. In 1860, at his instigation, the chair's title was changed to rhetoric and English literature, thus valorizing the study of English literature as an academic subject. The University of Edinburgh was the first university to institutionalize such a course. The Royal Commission of 1861, largely because of the success of Aytoun's lectures, recommended that the study of English literature be instituted at all of the Scottish universities and made a requirement for the M.A. degree. Because of the historic connection between logic and rhetoric, they decreed that it should be added to the responsibility of the professor of logic. Since professors often moved from one professorship to another, delivering the same lectures in both chairs, and because of the traditional connection between rhetoric and logic, the professors of logic and metaphysics are included in this study. The holders of the Regius Chair during the nineteenth century were the following:

1784	William Greenfield
1801	Andrew Brown
1835	George Moir
1840	William Spalding
1845	William Edmondstoune Aytoun
1865	David Masson

1895   George Saintsbury
1915   Herbert J. C. Grierson

The holders of the chair of logic and metaphysics included:

1786   James Finlayson
1808   David Ritchie
1836   Sir William Hamilton
1856   Alexander Campbell Fraser

Hugh Blair retired in 1784, having repeated the same lectures for his entire career and "having presumably nothing more to say" (Meikle 94). William Greenfield, Blair's assistant in the church of St. Giles, and Blair were appointed as joint professors of rhetoric and belles lettres, and in effect Greenfield took over the responsibility of the chair. We have only one set of student notes from Greenfield's course now preserved in the library at Aberdeen. He taught for fourteen years, and all we know of his teaching is its "disastrous end" when he was dismissed "for an offense unnamed though known to be immoral conduct" (Meikle 94), which Sir Alexander Grant in his history of the university called an "aberration of intellect." He was excommunicated from the church in 1798 and deprived of his chair and his degrees. Once again, the chair reverted to Blair. A syllabus of Greenfield's lectures appears in Arnot's *History of Edinburgh* published in 1803, and according to Henry W. Meikle, it "followed the lines laid down by his colleague Blair, but in an easier style, with illustrations drawn from a wider and contemporary field" (95).[3] Greenfield was highly respected before his dismissal, and in 1809, he published (anonymously) *An Essay on the Sources of the Pleasures Received from Literary Compositions*, based on his lectures.

    On Blair's death, the chair was offered to Sir Walter Scott, who declined it, and "probably to others who did not want it either" (Horn papers, EUL Ms. Gen. 1824, 8). It was finally accepted by Andrew Brown, another cleric at St. Giles, who was the last of the series of ministers to hold the professorship. We have no notes from his lectures, there are no publications recorded, and he is not included in the *Dictionary of National Biography*. His consuming interest was in the history of North America to which he devoted his life. His bulky manuscript is in the manuscript collection of the University of Edinburgh's library. It never found publication.

As a teacher, we know Brown through the rather rosy picture presented in Bower's *Guide,* a description possibly intended to attract students. In his evidence before the Royal Commissioners published in 1837, he comes off today as having been an uninspired and undemanding teacher, who really had no interest in his subject: "My class is not one of absolute necessity to the College and . . . the students." He did not "dare" to introduce examinations; essays were voluntary; and deciding on the prizes to be awarded had given him "a great deal of difficulty." When asked if he ascertained or enforced regular attendance, he replied that he had never yet "ventured upon any means of that kind." Obviously, Andrew Brown was more interested in his history of North America than in his rhetoric course. As a result of his lack of interest and the declining number of students, the commissioners recommended that the rhetoric class once again be united with logic. When Brown died, the government decided to follow the commissioners' suggestion by not filling the chair. There were protests from the college committee of the town council, who felt that the duties could not be appropriately added to any other chair and that the course could not be abandoned without great detriment to the university (Horn papers 12).

Consequently, George Moir was appointed to the Regius chair in 1835, the first of a series of advocates to hold the position. It was at this time that Carlyle applied for the chair and was turned down because of his publicly stated religious and political beliefs. This possibly explains Carlyle's attitude toward Moir, whom he called "little Georgie Moir" and described as a "dilettante . . . in all senses a neat man, in none a strong one" (qtd. in Meikle 98). Moir had broad-ranging interests and successfully managed to publish widely in both law and belles lettres; but possibly because he found himself spread too thinly, he resigned the chair after only five years.

William Spalding, the second advocate to hold the chair, did little to add to the luster of the course. He did institute a program requiring an essay every other week and two weekly examinations, one written and one oral. But, although the course was necessary for the M.A. degree, the only firm requirement was attendance at the lectures. He was a scholar of some note, and Horn remarks in his unpublished manuscript (1835) that "Shakespearean scholars continue to treat these works with respect, if no longer with enthusiasm." His treatise on rhetoric (1839) shows an understanding of his subject, and in his definition of rhetoric as a science, he reflects the sentiment of the day. His insistence that "a legitimate system of rhetoric would teach, not what eloquence is, but what it is not" prefigures I. A. Richards' defensive rhetoric. He apparently gave the impression during his five years at Edinburgh of an "over-conscientious and somewhat rigid instructor" (Meikle 100). In 1845, he accepted a position at the University of St. Andrews, where his teaching proved to be more successful in the small classes. Although a widely published scholar, he was not suited to the large public lectures at Edinburgh, where some sense of dramatic presence was necessary. Brown, Moir, and Spalding had done nothing to add to the chair, so hopefully formed under Hugh Blair. Attendance at the lectures seldom exceeded thirty-five students. The Regius chair had fallen into disrepute; as teachers, the holders of the chair were both uninteresting and, for the most part, uninterested.

The next holder of the chair, William Edmondstoune Aytoun, proved to be interested, interesting, and possessed of just the right dramatic flair for the University of Edinburgh's large public lectures. He was the third advocate in the chair, but unlike his predecessors who divided their interest and gave scant attention to the duties of the position, Aytoun took up his teaching responsibilities with vigor. Apparently, he did not dictate his lectures—we have no students' notes—but he did leave his extensive papers to the National Library of Scotland. Included in these are his lectures on rhetoric. It is obvious from these manuscripts that he wrote and rewrote his lectures with great care, constantly making changes. One note, dated 1858 on a lecture about sentences, states that "this lecture and the following must be rewritten." Another, on his lecture about formal rhetoric, states, "Good, but 8 last pages to be entirely rewritten." The changes are interesting and show how Aytoun adapted his lectures to the times and to his audience.[4]

Aytoun, like his predecessors in the chair, was trained for the bar, a vocation he never liked but pursued because of his father's insistence. He inherited from his mother his love of ballads

THE UNIVERSITY OF EDINBURGH

and poetry, and he is best known today in Scotland for his collection of ballads.[5] Like the dutiful Victorian son that he was, however, he worked hard at law, but his ideas are perhaps best expressed by the hero of his one novel, *Norman Sinclair*, who remarks, "I followed the law diligently, but somehow or other, I could never overtake it" (Meikle 101). He continued to maintain his interest in literature and became a frequent contributor to the journals of the day. In contrast to his predecessors, he appears, in pursuing his literary interests, to have had the chair in mind for some time. In a letter to his father, he wrote,

> You, perhaps unwillingly, touched in your last letter upon a subject which I have for some time contemplated, viz. a Chair in the University. The Chair of Belles Lettres, which in the time of Blair was the best attended in the College, must, in the common course of events, be vacant in the course of a few years. In its present state it is not likely that any very distinguished name will be found among the candidates, and if such should be the case, I shall make a push for it. I mention this chiefly to show you that I have an ultimate object in view in pursuing my literary studies. (Qtd. in Meikle 101)

Aytoun received the appointment in 1845 and proceeded to make the lectures one of the most popular in the university. Under his tenure, class attendance rose from 27 to 150. In a written response to the Royal Commissioners, he attributed the success of his class to the system of exercises that he introduced.

> So soon as I became aware of the deficiency of the students generally in vernacular composition, I adopted the method of prescribing to them a certain number of exercises upon subjects adapted to their capacity; all which were carefully revised by me; some times entirely rewritten, with notes and observations upon their styles, and returned to each student without public comment. (NLS MS 6913)

He complained to a friend that "I have as much MS. in the shape
of exercises as would roast an ox, to correct next week" (Martin
141). At one point, he hired a senior student, "a gentleman in
whose judgement and skill I could place entire confidence," but
added that he abandoned the practice because the students disliked
it and felt that "they were entitled to have the direct opinion of
the Professor" (NLS MS 6913).

The introductory lectures are probably the most interesting
for us since they give his ideas on education. He supported the
Scottish system of education and took "to task people who think
it beneath the dignity of a university 'to deal with rudimentary
elements' " (Frykman 22). He opposed the compulsory entrance
exams as excluding the poorer Scots. He insisted that one cannot
say to Scotsmen, "You are guilty of the sin of original poverty, let
it cleave to you to the grave" (qtd. in Frykman 23).

Certainly, he worked hard for a salary of one hundred
pounds, augmented by his class fees of three guineas per student,
with exemptions "in the cases of sons of Professors, or of poor
students with high certificates" (NLS MS 6913). But he felt that
the title of the chair was prejudicial to the attendance. "Many
persons entertain the idea that 'Rhetoric' is a trifling art, unsatisfac-
tory as a department of mental training, and that the term 'Belles
Lettres' signifies nothing more than general, and sometimes aim-
less criticism" (NLS MS 6913, 6). He described his own course
as consisting of four parts:

1. Vernacular Composition, comprehending the varieties and
niceties of style.
2. The leading rules for spoken discourse which includes the
principles of elocution, a subject which I regard as of vast
importance.
3. A series of ancient and medieval literature in so far only as it
affects ourselves.
4. A sketch of British literature.

He suggested that the course would be better named "English
Literature and Composition." Aytoun was successful. The Royal
Commissioners of 1858–62 doubled his salary, and it was then—

1860—that the chair was renamed the Regius Professorship of Rhetoric and English Literature.

Due to Aytoun's influence, English literature was officially recognized as an academic subject first in the University of Edinburgh, a development that was coeval with what was happening in the United States but was forty to fifty years ahead of Oxford and Cambridge. In view of Aytoun's success, the Royal Commissioners recommended that the other universities adopt a course in English literature and composition and that it be made compulsory for the M.A. degree, as it had been at Edinburgh since 1827.

The emphasis continued under Professor David Masson, the well-known Milton scholar who assumed the chair in 1865 after having been the professor of English literature at London University for thirteen years. Masson's course, newly entitled "Rhetoric and English Literature," is listed in the University of Edinburgh Calendar of 1866–67 as including three parts. The first part was to be a course of lectures on rhetoric, including "style and the more minute points of English composition," and the principles of literature. He divided the "methods of literature" into four parts: (1) historical and descriptive; (2) expository; (3) eloquence and oratorical literature; and (4) poetry and the literature of prose fiction. The second part of the course was to include lectures on the history of English literature. The third part of the course was to be "practical instruction in English Composition and in Reading and Speaking," to which Masson proposed to devote at least one meeting each week. The students were to write brief essays in class, which would be carefully "revised" (the same word that Aytoun used) and "returned to the students with such notes and hints as may seem most likely to be useful to them individually" (EUL Calendar 1866–67). The books listed for the course include Aristotle's *Rhetoric* and *Poetics* and Bain's *Composition and Rhetoric* and *English Grammar*.

Masson was not an inspired lecturer and appears to have spent his time on his own writings in English literature and particularly on his life of Milton, which became a classic in the field. He obviously dictated his lectures, which, in the students' notes, as stated earlier, appear to have been delivered unchanged for some thirty years. He did, however, have printed privately outlines of his notes, which are included with some manuscripts of students' notes (EUL Ms. Gen 1401–3).

Under the last holder of the chair, George Saintsbury, who was appointed in 1895, the course turned more and more toward literature. A prolific writer on the subject both of French and of English literature, his writings are prodigious. In 1896, he published his *History of Nineteenth-Century Literature*. The course, as described in the 1896 calendar, included a survey of style in poetry and prose from Chaucer to the nineteenth century on Mondays, Wednesdays, and Fridays; on Tuesdays and Thursdays, the lectures were to take for "text the books prescribed for the year," presumably literature. "A certain number of these Lectures will be specially devoted to the subject of Rhetoric, the texts being 'De Quincey's Essay,' with Whately's *Rhetoric*, Bain's *Composition and Rhetoric*, and Hodgson's *Errors in English* for illustration." In the description of the course, Saintsbury announced class examinations, in-class written exercises, and two longer written essays, "one before, one after Christmas."

Notes from Herbert J. C. Grierson's course are included here, since his lectures on rhetoric and composition are so clear and full. Also, he established the study of English literature at the University of Aberdeen, and it can be safely assumed that these lectures contain the gist of his lectures delivered at Aberdeen between 1894 and 1915. It is interesting that what is left of rhetoric has now become the responsibility of the professor of English literature.

By the end of the nineteenth century, English literature was well established at Edinburgh, with some remnants of rhetoric still included in the rhetoric and English literature course. Written work was still assigned, but because the universities were small, such written work was considered the responsibility of all of the arts professors, and the connection with rhetoric was becoming more and more tenuous. In general, the arts professors followed the recommendation of the *Report Made to His Majesty by a Royal Commission* in 1831: "In addition to Examinations, Exercises and Essays should be required from all the regular Students in each class, and ought to be criticized by the professor."

It should be noted that there was a course in rhetoric and

sermon writing in the divinity school, a course still very much in existence today. John Lee, who was later to become principal of the university, taught a course for divinity students from which there is a set of notes from 1821 (EUL Ms. Gen. DK. 88). This course is a fairly traditional rhetoric course with influences from the commonsense school of philosophy.

The Renaissance idea that logic was learned communication persisted into the nineteenth century, and there is clear evidence of this residue in the logic and metaphysics courses at the University of Edinburgh. The first course from which we have notes is that of James Finlayson, taken by the same John Lee just mentioned. Finlayson held the chair of logic from 1787 until his death in 1808. After an invective against the "primitive" philosophy, which was "very corrupt and absurd, and in many points even dangerous as it some times tended to lead the mind astray, and to sink it in the Valley of Obscurity, Doubt, and Uncertainty," the first three parts of his course dealt with logic, "commonly called Port Royal." The fourth part of the course, still a part of logic, was "an explanation of the most effectual means of conveying this truth to others with clearness and conviction." This section dealt with grammar and style and had little to do with rhetoric. He made a clear distinction between conveying information only, and "the desire to please and affect our hearers," and concluded that logic had only to do with the first (EUL Ms. Dc. 8.142/1–2).

David Ritchie took over the chair on the death of Finlayson in 1808 and held it for twenty-eight years. In the report of volume 1 of the evidence of the Royal Commission's visit of 1830, published in 1837, he was closely questioned about the historical connection between rhetoric and logic that might lead to repetition for the students in the courses. Ritchie has not come down through history as a favorite professor. He was described as a "tall, big-boned, strong man, with a powerful, rough voice, and great energy, though little polish, in his delivery" who was "more illustrious on the curling pond than in the Professorial Chair" (Grant 332). For these professors, rhetoric, or "the theory of language" as Ritchie called it, had by then become little more than grammar.

A person of a very different personality, Sir William Hamilton followed Ritchie in the chair in 1836. Under his tenure, the course became one in commonsense philosophy, which is now called psychology. There were four candidates for the chair, and his nomination was supported by M. Cousin with the following testimonial:

> What characterises Sir William Hamilton is precisely the Scottish intellect; and he is only attached to the philosophy of Reid and Stewart because their philosophy is the Scottish intellect itself applied to Metaphysics. Sir W. Hamilton never deviates from the highway of common sense. . . . Sir W. Hamilton knows all systems, ancient and modern, and he examines them by criticism of the Scottish intellect. (Qtd. in Grant 334)

Hamilton's emphasis was on philosophy, and he is generally considered a member of the Scottish school. His philosophy is best outlined in his *Lectures on Metaphysics and Logic* edited by H. L. Mansel and John Veitch. Hamilton gave two courses of lectures, one on psychology and philosophy, the other on logic. He was in the habit of writing his lectures the night before and seldom altering them afterwards as his students' notes indicate. He was widely respected and well liked; his classes were lively; and he frequently questioned his students by asking for summaries of his lectures. He was an effective teacher, but logic as part of rhetoric disappeared from his course and from that of Alexander Campbell Fraser, who was the last professor of logic and metaphysics in the century.

From this view of nineteenth-century rhetoric as it is included and excluded in various courses at the University of Edinburgh, several important trends can be traced. By the end of the century, the ancient rhetoric has not only been discarded but is gravely criticized and is being replaced by Francis Bacon, John Locke, David Hume, and by Thomas Reid's philosophy of common sense. Rhetoric becomes synonymous with criticism, and English literature enters academia. Used first as examples in the rhetoric/criticism course, it becomes ultimately worthy of its own study in courses in English literature. This development takes place first at the University of Edinburgh, and the other Scottish universities are forced by the Royal Commission to follow suit. English replaces Latin as the language of instruction and composition. Students still take Latin in the humanities course, but their reading and writing of Latin is no longer as important, as education takes on a pragmatic purpose by teaching the merchants of the city and by preparing students for their professional training in divinity, law, or medicine. What remains of rhetoric has become written composition—except in the divinity course, where oral delivery maintains its importance. Finally, composition, at the University of Edinburgh, becomes a shared responsibility in all arts courses. The composition course fails to develop in Scotland as it did in the United States for reasons that will become clearer later.

The University of Edinburgh: Archival Materials

The last set of notes from Herbert J. C. Grierson was taken at the University of Edinburgh in 1916–17. They are properly included here, but they may be presumed to be similar to his lectures at the University of Aberdeen where he held the Chalmers Chair of English from 1893 until 1915 when he moved to the University of Edinburgh. In the citations that follow, the professor's name and the years of his professorship are followed by the library in which the manuscript is located, its call number, and any pertinent information about its condition, such as legibility, number of pages, if it is paginated, or volumes. Libraries are abbreviated as follows: EUL, University of Edinburgh Library; GUL, University of Glasgow Library; AUL, University of Aberdeen Library; and NLS, National Library of Scotland. The exact inscription on the title page then follows in italics. The manuscripts are listed in chronological order under the course title within which they were taught.

Rhetoric, Belles Lettres, and English Literature

GREENFIELD, WILLIAM. 1784–1801. AUL MS 189. 120 pages. Good copy. *Notes from a Course of Lectures upon Belles Lettres*

*delivered by William Greenfield at the University of Edinburgh in
the Years 1785–6 from November 22 1785 to April 19 1786.*
On the last page there is a note: "A course of 53 lectures
begun Tuesday, November 22 1785—Terminated abruptly
on account of W. Greenfield's health on Wednesday, April
12 1786." Starts with a defense of criticism, stating that
"genius would despise and overlook the rules." These notes
follow closely the general outline of Hugh Blair's lectures.

MOIR, GEORGE. 1835–40. GUL MS Gen. BC17-x.13, No. 10.
14-page printed pamphlet. No author listed. Good condition.
Introductory Lecture to the Course of Rhetoric and Belles Lettres.
Edinburgh: Printed by John Stark, 1835.
This is the introductory lecture of George Moir when
he was appointed to the chair of rhetoric and belles lettres
at the University of Edinburgh in 1835, a chair he occupied
for five years. He admits in his opening paragraph that he
has been able to spend only "a few months" on a "subject
that might well have demanded the labour of years" (1). This
is, in Moir's case, not a rhetorical ploy but a fact, even though
he outlines the subject of the course as "literature in general,
comprehending under that term not only Poetry and Eloquence, but all those written productions of the human mind
which appeal in any shape to the imagination" (1). He sees
as its object to "furnish us . . . with sound rules of criticism
and composition" but also indirectly to "familiarize us with
noble thoughts and pure emotions, to refine our taste and
feelings, to elevate our pursuits and views of duty; to supply
morality with additional assistance, and sorrow with another
source of consolation and support" (1).
He continues by saying that the tone of criticism has
changed in the eighteenth century. Where the eighteenth-
century critic was always "the stern and dignified Judge," the
critic of the nineteenth century stands as "the interpreter
between the inspired and the uninspired" (6). He continually
equates rhetoric, the principles of criticism, and the practical
rules of composition with the study of literature. He maintains that the writers who will remain permanently popular
are those who "have laboured to raise, rather than depress,

71

the spirit and hope of men." Thus, he says, Voltaire has "already shrunk into a narrow room," and Lord Byron will probably "occupy but a small place in the hearts and memories of the next generation" (11). He concludes that genuine literature is the essence of religion, philosophy, and art—of all that speaks to the immortal part of man.

SPALDING, WILLIAM. 1840–45. EUL MS Gen. 769D. 12 essays. Handwriting large and clear, binding fragile. *Class Essays with Comments by William Spalding, Professor of Rhetoric and Belles Lettres, Edinburgh University, 1844–5 by John Dick Peddies, Matric. 1839–44.*

A collection of twelve essays, varying in length from twelve pages (with wide margins) to forty-two pages, written between November 16, 1844, and March 26, 1845, by a student in his last year at the university in the course in rhetoric and belles lettres.

The subjects of the essays provide a good indication of the course content; several are, in fact, entitled reports of lectures. The first essay is entitled "Remarks on Harris' Treatise on Music, Painting, and Poetry"; the second is a report of part of the lectures on Grecian literature; the third covers the reasons why Roman literature was entirely the result of imitation of Grecian models; the fourth is "On Disposition"; the fifth is a report on Spalding's first lecture on the Middle Ages, "with a few preliminary remarks on the decline of Roman literature." On January 10, there is an essay reporting on the second lecture on the second period of modern English literature. Essay 9 contains an abstract of a speech followed by a rhetorical analysis of it. This appears to be an essay written in class since the student speaks several times of his inability to make certain points because of a lack of time. Essay 10 is a copy of a speech on the question of the connection between church and state, followed by an essay on the want of principle in architectural criticism. The last essay, forty-five pages long, is entitled "Remarks on Different Points in the Association Theory of Beauty." The student acknowledges having used his lecture notes as one of the authorities consulted. It is clear from these essays that Spal-

ding included Greek, Roman, and English literature in his
course, as well as the principles of rhetoric largely based on
the Scottish philosophy.

Spalding's comments, not lengthy and generally complimentary of this student's work, are probably complemented
by oral comments. He corrects some grammatical errors,
such as agreement and the use of *will* for *shall*, and he marks
misspellings that do not seem to have changed much in a
century: *principle* for *principal* and *their* for *there*. These essays
tell us a great deal about the content of Spalding's course.

SPALDING, WILLIAM. 1840–45. GUL BC 28-d.13. "Treatise on
Rhetoric." Printed book, good condition. *Treatise on Rhetoric,
in Treatises on Poetry, Modern Romance, and Rhetoric; Being
the Articles under Those Heads, Contributed to the Encyclopaedia
Britannica*. 7th ed. Edinburgh: Adam and Charles Black, 1839.

This treatise is included with two treatises by George
Moir also written for the Encyclopaedia Britannica. Since I
could find no notes from Spalding's lectures, either his own
or his students', this treatise is the only record of Spalding's
views on rhetoric. It is a full, detailed, and easily readable
account.

In his introduction, Spalding asserts that "rhetoric has
been put under the ban of the empire of literature" because
truth, good taste, and eloquence are "the antithesis of rhetoric" (276). "A legitimate system of rhetoric would teach, not
what eloquence *is*, but what it is *not*" (277). He urges the
study of literary works as models and emphasizes the value
of practice. Like all of his contemporaries, he speaks of
rhetoric as a "science," not a primary science but one that
rests on the rational systems of psychology, logic, and ethics.
Part 2 of chapter 1 includes a classical discussion of Logos,
ethos, and pathos cast in modern terminology: "The Production of Belief by Arguments" (307), "The Production of
Belief by Impressions" (330), and "The Production of Belief
by Excited Emotion" (332). Chapter 2 is a traditional treatment of arrangement; chapter 3, "The Principles of Style,"
while acknowledging the works of the ancients, also includes
suggestions from George Campbell, Hugh Blair, Lord

Kames, and Richard Whately. Part 3, "Criticism of Rhetoric," draws from ancient and modern political oratory. This is a traditional treatment of rhetoric with new terminology, although classical terms are retained in the section on arrangement. The works of contemporary English writers are included in the section on style.

AYTOUN, WILLIAM EDMONDSTOUNE. 1845–64. NLS MS 4910. 175 pages. Lecture Notes. Six lectures written by Aytoun, three on rhetoric, three on the structure of sentences. Binding good. Handwriting fairly clear and readable. Paginated by a later hand.

This manuscript is part of the extensive holdings in the National Library of Scotland of material by William Edmondstoune Aytoun. The holdings include accounts, lectures, and correspondence. NLS MS 4897 includes his constantly revised and rewritten introductory lectures beginning in 1856. NLS MSS 4898–4908 contain his lectures on poetry. NLS MS 4907 is on Scottish and European ballads. NLS MSS 4910–11 are his lectures on "Formal Rhetoric." NLS MS 4914 contains class lists and student themes; and NLS MS 4928 contains Aytoun's outline for a treatise on public speaking (see Lunsford 327–35).

This first lecture on formal rhetoric, written by Aytoun, although proposing to cover classical rhetoric, is, in fact, largely a criticism of the ancient system. Aytoun divides the system into four parts, omitting memory: discovery or invention of arguments, arrangement of arguments, style, and delivery. "The ancients," he asserts, "applied their ingenuity chiefly to the first two branches. The moderns, I think with great propriety, give prominence and precedence to the others, as being by far the most useful and practical, and the best suited to the wants and requirements of the age" (4).

The first lecture, delivered in 1851, is largely a criticism of the topics, with only a short paragraph devoted to the nature of the audience. Ethos, the character of the speaker, is omitted entirely. He asserts that the "artificiality of the system seems most apparent in Invention" and repeats his opinion of "the utter worthlessness of the art" (7). He invokes a long quotation from William Spalding, his predecessor in the chair, to reinforce his criticism of the commonplaces (12–13).

Aytoun continues to outline the traditional precepts of rhetoric even while criticizing them, asserting that the ancients and some moderns have made "rhetoric appear distasteful by encumbering it with artificial rules, and those in such number, that were we to observe them all, our speech would degenerate into a tissue of woven sophistry" (63). He then expresses his admiration for Hugh Blair, "who may be called the founder of modern rhetoric in this country, in getting rid of much of the cumbersome precepts of antiquity, and in laying down no more than broad and simple rules, which everyone can understand, for composition" (63).

In spite of his plea for simple rules, he devotes three long lectures to the structure of sentences after his lecture on the "Conduct of a Discourse," which treats the proof of an argument.

MASSON, DAVID. 1865–95. EUL MS Gen. 1401–3. 3 volumes, each paginated separately: vol. 1, 109 pp.; vol. 2, 77 pp.; vol. 3, 131 pp. Handwriting clear, ink slightly faded, binding in good condition. Insert marked "Privately Printed" outlines in detail the five periods of English literature covered in Masson's lectures. *Notes of English Literature: From Lectures on Rhetoric and English Literature by Prof. Masson.* Taken by J. Allan Gray. Session 1868–69.

Volumes 1 and 2 cover English literature. Volume 3, entitled "Rhetoric and the Principles of Literature," outlines the periods prior to the English period (mythical, Roman, Anglo-Saxon, and Anglo-Norman) and emphasizes their influence on the literature of England. Each period is preceded by a short historical overview.

1. 1250–1400 (1:66–68). Covers in some detail the major writers of the period: John Barbour, "the father of Scottish Verse," William Langland, John Gower, and Geoffrey Chaucer.
2. 1400–1580 (1:88–101). Masson covers this period briefly, giving more attention to the history than to the

literature. In discussing the poetry of the period, he mentions a number of Scottish poets, saying that they "are superior to their English contemporaries, and are more like Chaucer" (1:100).

3. 1580–1625 (1:101–2:38). Mentions as the main writers of this period, which he covers in some detail, Edmund Spenser; Sir Philip Sidney; Lord Francis Bacon; William Shakespeare; Ben Jonson; Archbishop Usher of Arnmagh; and John Selden. He gives his main attention to Spenser (1:106–2:5) and to Shakespeare (2:5–2:26).

4. 1625–1688 (2:38–65). Gives primary attention to John Milton (2:50–60) and John Dryden (2:60–64).

5. 1688–1725 (2:65–75). Divides the authors of the period "according to the field of literature in which they chose to exhibit their talents" (2:63): in history; in science and philosophy; in oratory and exposition; and in imagination or poetry, in which he includes the novelists, the dramatists, and the poets (2:68–72).

6. 1789 to the Present (2:68–78). This period is covered in just over one page. No writer is mentioned. This and the fifth period are covered very sketchily, with more attention given to English history than to literature.

Volume 3 covers "Rhetoric and the Principles of Literature," beginning with various definitions of rhetoric.

Hobbes says it is, "that Faculty by which we understand what will serve our turn to win belief." Aristotle regards Rhetoric as the art of public speaking and persuasion. . . . Modern writers have taken a wider view of it. "Eloquence," says Whately "is now almost as often applied to writing as to speaking." Rhetoric may be as appropriately applied to the production of the poet as to that of the orator. This more nearly corresponds with the view of Rhetoric taken by Campbell, and Blair, who under that head discuss wit, taste, humour, imagination, narrative writing, etc. (Flyleaf of vol. 3)

Masson then gives his own definition: "Rhetoric is the art of effective writing and speaking; the Science of the laws which relate thought to expression; the Science of the style, and principles of Literature; the Science of Literature" (3:1). He asks his students to note that "Rhetoric is either a Science or an Art. Rhetoric as being the expression of the State of mind from which it proceeded is a Science but Rhetoric looked upon as the manner of expression is an Art, giving rules all of which are derived from rhetoric as a science" (3:1). He divides literature into four classes: the historical, the expository, the oratorical, and the literature of the imagination. He then moves to a traditional description of the figures of speech (3:5–15), followed by a discussion of style and composition (3:16–27). Under the second heading, Masson defines style: "To change your style, you must also change the manner of your thought. Style, then, is thought" (3:17). "Presupposing grammatical correctness," he delineates five features of good style: intelligibility, nonoffensiveness, vivacity, artistic beauty, and richness or exuberance (3:21–26). The remainder of the third volume is a discussion of the four kinds of literature. Under historical literature, narration and description are treated in detail (3:28–65). Expository literature (3:66–79) is defined as "didactic or scientific. . . . whose function is explanation" (3:66). He lists orderliness, clearness, and impressiveness as qualities of this kind of literature (3:73).

Oratorical literature, the longest of the four sections (3:80–105), is defined as "argumentative, persuasive, controversial, and practical" (3:80) and includes both spoken and written. He begins with an overview of Aristotle's *Rhetoric* with a short index and concludes with a description of the principles of classical rhetoric in general.

The final section, poetical literature (3:106–31), begins with two theories of poetry—Aristotle's and Bacon's—which he then reconciles. He defines imagination as a form of poetic cognition, "the bringing of mental materials into new combinations" (3:113). This definition is followed by a discussion of memory: the upper memory and the under memory. This section on poetical literature concludes with a section on how a poet should be criticized (3:120–23) with such questions as "Is he a poet?" "Of what worth is he

THE UNIVERSITY OF EDINBURGH

as a poet?" "In what kind of circumstance does he excel as a poet?" "In what emotional key is his poetry?" and finally, "What proportion is extra Poetic?" He divides prose into the prose ode, the novel, and prose drama and verse into lyric, epic, and dramatic poetry (3:123). He concludes by discussing the relation between verse and prose.

MASSON, DAVID. 1865–95. EUL MS Gen. 2076. No pagination, contents, or readily observable outlines or divisions. Handwriting clear, binding broken. *Professor Masson's Lectures on English Literature. Session 1878–79.*

This is the only set of notes that covers the last period of English literature (1789 to the present) in any detail (twelve pages). Masson asks his students to "note the wonderful influx of the new scientific conception and its effect on the literature of this period," adding, "We live in the wake of the French Revolution." He claims that Robert Burns "sank into Scotland as never before did lyrist into the heart of a people. After Burns it was impossible for any British poet merely to continue the old style." This emphasis on Burns and his influence on Lord Byron, William Wordsworth, and Samuel Taylor Coleridge appears for the first time in Masson's lectures.

MASSON, DAVID. 1865–95. EUL MS Dk. 1.3.2. 22 pages. Second volume paginated with précis. Handwriting is clear, binding good. *Masson's Lectures (1879–80) (The Critical Course) taken by William K. Dickson.*

The first page contains a useful précis of the lectures.

General definitions—1 Tropes and Figures; Primary tropes, 2; Secondary tropes, 3; Figures of thought, 4; of diction, 5–6; Criticism, 7; Qualities of Style in general, 8–9

Historical Literature. General principles, 9–11; Voyages and travels, diaries, etc., 11; Biography, 12; History proper, 12–13

Expository Literature. Definition, 14; Positive Science, 14; Philosophic and Speculative, 14–15; General Characteristics, 15–16

Oratorical Literature. Definition, 14; Ancient Rhetoric, 16–19; Remarks and Classification of speeches,
19–20.
Poetry or Literature of the Imagination. 20, 21, 22.
Shakespeare and Elizabethan Literature: n.p.

Under criticism, Masson offers a series of critical adjectives applicable to all primary thought about matter: true-
false, able-stupid, original-commonplace, deep-shallow, im-
passioned-unimpassioned, poetical-prosaic, calm-vehement,
fine-coarse, and so on. In other respects, this set of notes
does not appear to differ in any significant way from the
1868–69 set by J. Allan Gray, although they were delivered
twelve years later. They are less detailed than the earlier set
of notes.

MASSON, DAVID. 1865–95. EUL MS Dk. 4.28–31. 4 volumes.
Paginated. Vols. 1–3 contain 221 pp. of notes on English
literature. Vol. 4, entitled *Theoretical Course, i.e. Rhetoric, Style,
and the Principles of Literature*, contains 85 pp. Handwriting
clear at beginning but deteriorates toward the end, binding
good. *Rhetoric and English Literature. Historical Course. i.e. History of English Literature including History of English Language.
Session 1881–82. Taken by George J. Lumsden.*
These lecture notes do not differ in any significant way
from the 1868–69 notes. Pasted to the back inside cover is
an article from *The Scotsman*, dated Wednesday, October 26,
1881, with summaries of lectures delivered by Professors
David Masson (English literature), Alexander Campbell Fraser (logic and metaphysics), and the professors of Greek and
moral philosophy. All lectures, according to the article, were
greeted with "applause" except Professor Masson's, which
was greeted with "Loud Applause." On the inside of the last
page of volume 4 are essay and exam assignments. There are
two essay assignments:

1. Probationary of preliminary essay on "The Wandering
   Minstrel." It is not to consist of more than 1200 words.
   Attend to *neatness of form, expression and pointing, as well*

79

as the matter. Assigned on November 18 to be given in on December 2.
2. First Competitive Essay on "The History of English Blank Verse" given out December 16 to consist of not more than 2,000 words. Given in on February 3.

There are 2 exams, one on December 21, the other on February 15.

MASSON, DAVID. 1865–95. EUL Dc. 5.100–102. 3 volumes. 55 lectures. Paginated. Handwriting clear, binding good. *Rhetoric and English Literature. Lectures by Prof. Masson. Session 1882–83. By Andrew David Sloan.*
Volume 1 is titled *Theoretical* and treats rhetoric. Volumes 2 and 3 cover a history of English literature. These notes are less detailed, but they are otherwise almost identical to the 1868–69 notes, often matching word for word.

MASSON, DAVID. 1865–95. NLS MS 6652. 8 lectures. Paginated in another hand. Headings clearly marked. Handwriting large and clear, ink faded, binding good. *Rhetoric I and English Literature. Prof. Masson. Edinbro' 'Varsity.* Session 1881–82. Notes taken by J. M. Barrie.
This manuscript is noteworthy because it is signed by J. M. Barrie, the well-known playwright. It includes only the rhetoric section of the course.
Lecture 1 begins with the sentence: "The Rhetorical course on which we enter today includes *rhetoric, style, and the principles of literature.*" Masson then begins with his customary definition of rhetoric: "the old and restricted definition," and "the wider and more modern definition" (2). After giving the definitions of Aristotle and Quintilian, he gives the "medium definition" of Whately: "the art of argumentative composition." He then lists a number of modern definitions:

George Campbell: "the art of adapting speech to its ends"
Hugh Blair: "includes tragedy, comedy, wit, humour, etc."
Alexander Bain: "discusses the means whereby language, spoken or written, may be rendered effective"

David Masson: "the Art and Science of all literary expression"

"Whately has observed that the invention of the printing press necessarily led to an extension of the meaning of such words as Rhetoric, and eloquence of written matter should be added to that of public speaking" (4). Campbell includes poetry; Blair includes more (6). But, Masson continues, it does not matter which definition is used since, according to the modern sense, both rhetoric in its old sense and literature generally "are included under the one word 'Rhetoric' " (6). He then follows with the definition of literature that has appeared in all of his students' notes.

It is the past and present thought and feeling of the world as it is preserved or capable of being preserved in written language, and is found chiefly in books. For a physical conception of the literature of a country or the world imagine all its books lying in one stupendous pile, or in an enormous library. (2)

Note that Masson includes here only written work under the category of literature, while in his earlier notes he insists that "rhetoric is the art of effective writing and speaking." Masson then makes his usual classifications of literature based on "the moods of the human mind." The remainder of this set of lectures covers "Style and Composition" (14–83)—a more detailed treatment than in the J. Allan Gray notes taken eleven years before. "The ancients' division of intellect was into 3 parts, viz. *memory, reason, and imagination* as if human intellect were a house with 3 such chambers. This division is confusing and it is more advisable to look upon the 3 moods as affecting us at various times" (14). He suggests the following readings from the moderns:

Lord Kames' Elements of Literature
Campbell's Philosophy of Rhetoric
Blair's Lectures
Whately's Rhetoric (Pt. 3)

81

Coleridge
Herbert Spencer
Dean Alford
Bain
Seeley and Abbott
—also Errors in Use of English by Hodgson. (16)

He then includes a long section on figures and tropes (17–58), followed by an interesting section, "Rhetorical Analysis," in which he clarifies the use of figures and tropes (58–59). He underlines the following sentence: *"All the so-called tropes and figures of speech are when strictly considered tropes and figures of thought—varieties of mental action, manoeuvres of the mind in the act of thinking, modifications in the very substance of the thought"* (59). The last lecture, on style and criticism, starts with the thought that "expression is coequal with mental power and a measure of that power" (62). He adds, several pages later,

> In other words, we might say that the process of expression is the process of thinking out something that is vaguely existing in the mind, or the assembling of images from all parts of the mind into verbal expression. . . . There is thus in theory an absolute identity between style or expression or diction and thought. (65)

The section on criticism is similar to the other sets of notes and offers little that is new or enlightening. He suggests that a "perusal of the whole of a writer's works generally suggests one predominant or pervading impression and a sufficient interpretation of this is a high office of the *critic*." Although he says that "no able critic would think of making any mechanical apparatus to help him yet such might be drawn up by arranging in parallel columns opposing adjectives of primary thought." Thus, able versus stupid, deep versus shallow, and so on through the list that he has offered in all of his lectures. After a section on primary and subsidiary

82

thought, he concludes with a section on grammatical correctness (74).

This set of notes is clear, easy to read, and shows a shift in his conception of oratorical literature as excluding speech and including only written language—derived from his new definition of literature.

MASSON, DAVID. 1865–95. EUL MS Gen. 1863–64. 2 volumes. Not paginated, divisions are unclear, handwriting and binding good. *English Literature taken by Miss Penelope Gordon Watson. (1888–89)*.

These notes, one of the few sets I found that were taken by a woman, begin with the lecture on rhetoric very much as it appears in other sets of notes with, however, the omission of the long definition of rhetoric so prominent in the earlier lectures. Delivered twenty-three years after Masson assumed the chair, these notes differ little from the first set of notes taken twenty years earlier in 1868.

Logic and Metaphysics

FINLAYSON, JAMES. 1786–1808. EUL MS Dc. 8.142/1–2. 2 volumes. Paginated by volume. Handwriting is erratic but usually clear, ink is brown, binding is good. Vol. 1: *Notes from the Lectures of Professor Finlayson on Logic*. Taken by John Lee, 1795–96.

These notes, taken by John Lee, who later became principal of the University of Edinburgh, contain much overwriting, crossing out, and correction. Volume 1 is a straightforward history of philosophy, with sixty pages on Greek and Roman philosophy. A new title page, *A System of Logic in Four Parts*, begins with new page numbers and proceeds very much in the manner of Finlayson's other lecture notes. The sentences are complete, and there are no crossed out sections, indicating that these are dictates.

Vol. 2: *Notes from the Lectures of Professor Finlayson on Logic*. Taken by John Lee, 1796–97.

Volume 2 is entitled *Logic—Part 2* and is the course referred to in EUL MS Gen. 774–78D. "In this branch of the course, we intend to give an enumeration and arrangement of the general principles which pervade every part of our knowledge and [by] which it may be all resolved." He begins by surveying the general principles by which we organize knowledge and then moves on to describe the three ways in which knowledge can help us attain general principles: by examining simple general elements common to all individuals, by fixing on general characteristics, and by examining individual characteristics. In this section, he covers ontology, the general notions that are common to every human thought; "Of Mind"; and "Of the General Attributes of Matter." Part 2 is called "Cosmology" (42), and part 3 is titled "Encyclopedology"—the knowledge "that we have of these objects" (52). On page 60, there is a section entitled "Philosophy," which concludes with a section called "Art." These notes are very confused and are of interest to the scholar of rhetoric only as they suggest what is offered in Finlayson's second logic course.

FINLAYSON, JAMES. 1786–1808. EUL MS Gen. 774–78D. 5 volumes. Paginated by volume, with tables of contents, elaborately scrolled title pages, and four clear divisions. Writing very clear, binding good. *An Epitome of Logic, Delivered in Lectures in the University of Edinburgh by James Finlayson, A.D.P.* Taken by David Pollock, 1796–97.

This is a clear, well-organized set of notes taken by a conscientious student from a structured set of lectures, which were probably dictated. There is a detailed table of contents with short summaries of the four parts and the chapters within the parts.

Part 1, entitled "Analysis of the Human Understanding," continues through volume 2. After a polemic against the "corrupt and absurd and in many Points even dangerous" philosophy of the primitive philosophers, Finlayson moves to how Bacon, "seeing the imperfect Waste of Philosophy—that part of it called Logic in particular," prepared the way for a new system (2:4). The second lecture begins with logic, "commonly called Port Royal," and is divided into four parts:

1. An analysis of the human understanding.
2. A classification of the Objects to which the Powers of the understanding are directed.
3. An explanation of the best Method of employing these Powers in the Discovery of Truth.
4. An Explanation of the most effectual Means of conveying this Truth to others with Clearness and Conviction.

Of these four, the first, third, and fourth are considered in this course; the second is reserved for another, which is designed for those who attend a second year. He defines logic as "the science or art which teaches the Method of discovering Truth, and of conveying that Truth to others with clearness and precision, or, as being both a Science and an Art, may be defined, the Science of human Thought and the Art of conveying that Science to others." The first chapter then treats perception and sensation through an examination of the five senses and subsequently consciousness, conception, memory, and abstraction, which includes genus and species. The second volume treats in turn judgment, imagination, reasoning, taste, and the moral sense, or faculty, and the power of will.

Part 2 is left for another course, and part 3 is entitled "An Explanation of the Best Method of Employing the Powers of the Understanding in the Discovery of Truth" and continues through volume 3 and part of volume 4. It treats in order seven kinds of evidence—that derived from intellection, from physical evidence, from common sense, from memory, from testimony, from experience, and from analogy. Part 3 concludes with the sources of errors explained in terms of Bacon's "Idols of the Tribe," the "Den," the "Market," and the "Theatre."

Part 4 is entitled "An Explanation of the Most Effectual Means of Conveying Truth to Others with Clearness and Conviction" and continues through the remainder of volumes 4 and 5. After a brief view of the means "which men have made use of to communicate their thoughts to each other," he moves into a brief overview of words and sentences with an emphasis on grammar. The largest portion of this section is devoted to

85

those qualities of style that fit it "for the communication of thought with clearness and perspicuity" (5:15). Here Finlayson makes an interesting distinction between logic and rhetoric. He says, in the use of speech, there are two objects—first, "to convey information or instruction, or secondly, to unite with this, the desire to please and affect our hearers" (5:15). He then asserts that it is the first of these only "that we have to do here" (5:16). The lectures then treat the three qualities of good style—perspicuity, clearness, and conviction—which are discussed at length.

He concludes with the "rules of language" (5:58–59). The conclusion, pages 75 to 160 of volume 5, is a lengthy and detailed review of the matter covered in the course.

FINLAYSON, JAMES. 1786–1808. NLS MS 3530. Paginated. Includes only lectures 27–50. Ink faded, binding weak. *Notes from Dr. Finlayson's Lectures on Logic by John C. Colquhoun from January 22 to April 7 1800.*

These notes differ markedly from others by Finlayson. After a discussion of taste, which is divided into sensibility, correctness, and refinement, Finlayson concludes that "these qualities when united would give us the idea of the perfect critic" (5). The second part of the course is divided into three parts: the nature of truth and evidence, the means by which evidence is to be obtained, and the sources of error that lead us away from truth. After the briefest mention of evidence from common sense, Finlayson covers the classical concepts of the syllogism, the enthymeme, the prosyllogism, and the epicheirema, concluding with induction after Bacon. There is a brief section describing cases where the syllogism is not applicable and describing methods of analysis and synthesis. The lectures conclude with a short history of language.

There is none of the usual invective against Aristotle or discussion of the syllogism as faulty that characterize Finlayson's other lectures.

FINLAYSON, JAMES. 1786–1808. EUL MS Gen. 1379–81. 3 volumes. Paginated with careful indexes. Handwriting clear but faded, binding good. *Notes on Logic—Being the Substance of a*

Course of Lectures on That Subject. Taken by Archibald Alison—
Academiae: Edinensis. 1807–8.

This set of notes was delivered the year of Finlayson's
death, and, although the last volume records that the lectures
were delivered by both Dr. Finlayson and a Dr. Baird, they
were probably the lectures of Finlayson that were read by
Baird.

Volume 1—November 12, 1807. There are six introductory lectures, followed by twenty-six on pneumatology,
heavily influenced by commonsense philosophy, with the
usual invective against Aristotle. "The Logic of Aristotle . . .
is full of error and in some places perhaps injurious" (2).

Volume 2—January 5, 1808. The second volume contains twenty-five lectures: eleven on pneumatology, six on
evidence, and five on the syllogism.

Volume 3—February 19, 1808. The discussion of the
syllogism is continued, and pages 41–97 cover the "communication of thoughts." Finlayson states that "writing is by
far the best and most expeditious" of the signs used to
communicate to men at a distance and is superior to voice
and gesture. He moves to a consideration of the parts of
speech, the forming of good sentences, the several matters
of style (perspicuity, vivacity, dignity, and harmony), and
the framing of a discourse.

These notes are clear, easy to follow, well indexed, and
reflect the logic courses of the time. Communication—so-
called instead of rhetoric—is treated as part of logic. There
is no actual use of the word *rhetoric* throughout the lectures,
and they are heavily influenced by the commonsense school
of philosophy.

RITCHIE, DAVID. 1808–1836. EUL MS Gen. Dc. 5.20–21. 2
volumes. No pagination or table of contents. Handwriting is
almost illegible. There is no title page. The first page is headed,
"November 1, 1809: Logic and Rhetoric."

I did not attempt to read this very difficult manuscript,
but it is interesting to note the word *rhetoric* in the title.

RITCHIE, DAVID. 1808–1836. EUL MS Gen. 1720. 344 pp.
Lectures date from November to April 10. Paginated, hand-

writing clear, binding good. *Notes of Dr. D. Ritchie's Lectures on Logic University of Edinburgh. Session 1823/4. Taken by JM.*
A notation before the first lecture reads: "Nota.—The whole of these notes were written several hours and sometimes longer after the lectures were delivered. This must be attended to in any reliance that might be placed in their correctness. (signed) J.M."

Logic, according to Dr. Ritchie, is to be "considered as an art rather than a science, viz. the art of using our reason aright and of communicating truth to others, and of avoiding error" (3).

In the second lecture, Dr. Ritchie insists that this study "has no connection with Pneumatology which concerns spirits nor with any which regards man as a moral agent. This last is commonly called 'ethics.'" The course follows the normal sequence of the logic in the school of common sense, with emphasis on perception through the five senses. There is a fifty-page introduction on the history of philosophy. He ranks Sir Isaac Newton as "the greatest modern philosopher" (52). After mention of John Locke and his faults, he discusses David Hume and Thomas Reid, concluding that "the human mind was long enveloped in a cloud which however was at last dispelled" and that "in the present day, philosophy has attained to as high a pitch as it ever attained at any former period" (55). After this introduction, the course does not differ much from the approach of Finlayson. The last thirty pages are devoted to a "Theory of Language" (345–74), which is little more than a review of grammar.

HAMILTON, SIR WILLIAM. 1836–56. EUL MS Gen. 49D. 856 pp. Handwriting clear, but student shorthand makes reading difficult. Binding good. *Notes of Lectures on Logic by Sir William Hamilton. 1847–48. Taken by D. McLaren.*
Toward the end, the student abandons many of his shorthand symbols. There is an elaborate table of contents and a careful ten-page index. The last ten pages cover the communication of knowledge. Rhetoric is not mentioned in the index.

HAMILTON, SIR WILLIAM. 1836–56. GUL MS Gen. 101 1/2. 2 volumes. Vol. 1 is missing; vol. 2 has 185 pp.; vol. 3 is not paginated. Handwriting difficult to read, binding good. *Metaphysical Lectures by Sir William Hamilton. Taken by John I. Kelton. Session 1848–49.*
    On the title page of these notes, there is the couplet

On Earth there is nothing great but Man
In Man there is nothing great but mind.

    This is a hard-to-read, incomplete set of notes. The more accessible printed version, edited by John Veitch and the Rev. H. L. Mansel, is more reliable. (See GUL E 3/4-z.13–16.)

HAMILTON, SIR WILLIAM. 1836–56. NLS MS 9166. 181 pp. Lectures 21–35. Index. Writing small but clear, binding good. *Lectures of Sir William Hamilton on Logic, Commencing November 4, 1851. Taken by William Carstares Dunlop. Volume Second.*
    It is clear from the nature of these notes that Sir William Hamilton, like many other professors of the period, dictated his lectures. The following sentence from this set of notes could only have been taken down from a lecturer who was reading slowly and with frequent pauses for the benefit of the students.

The explanation of this, I may observe, that as the distinctness of a concept is contained in the clear apprehension of the parts that make up its whole or sum; and as it is the sum of these attributes in two opposite relations which constitute two opposite wholes, and as these wholes are severally capable of explanation by analysis, it follows that each of these expositions will contribute its peculiar share to the general distinctness of the concept. (4)

The first twelve pages cover the quality of concepts; pages 13–22 discuss how concepts relate to each other. What follows is a close explanation of the categories. All of this material is taken, as Hamilton asserts, from Aristotle's *Organon*. Hamilton notes that Aristotle has "been arbitrarily and abusively perverted" by modern philosophers (23). This set of notes has a number of elaborate diagrams, including one that illustrates a concept very much like Sheridan Baker's keyhole (179).

HAMILTON, SIR WILLIAM. 1836–56. GUL E 3/4-z.13–16. 4 volumes. Excellent indexes at ends of vols. 2 and 4. Printed books in good condition. *Lectures on Metaphysics and Logic by Sir William Hamilton, Bart.*, edited by the Rev. H. L. Mansel and John Veitch. 4 vols. Edinburgh and London: William Blackwood and Sons, 1870.

These lectures, published after Hamilton's death and coedited by a former student, H. L. Mansel, and by a former assistant, John Veitch, are compiled from the original lecture notes and the lecture notes of students. They are filled out with notes extracted from Hamilton's commonplace book. The editors describe Hamilton's well-known habit of writing his lectures during the "currency of the sessions." Hamilton delivered three lectures a week, so each lecture was usually written "on the day, or more properly, on the evening and night, preceding its delivery" (x). Hamilton's philosophy is heavily influenced by the Scottish school, especially the association of ideas. Anyone interested in Hamilton's work would do well to look at the detailed tables of contents and indexes to determine which parts are of special interest.

FRASER, ALEXANDER CAMPBELL. 1856–91. EUL MS Gen. 2057–58. 2 volumes. Handwriting is clear. *Notes Taken in the Junior Class of Logic and Metaphysics by E. Monteith Macphail during Session 1880–1881. A. Campbell Fraser, L.L.D. Professor.* The first volume contains nine "Introductory Lectures," dated October 29, 1880, to November 12, 1880; the second volume (entitled "volume 1") is dated November 15, 1880, to January 28, 1881. Fraser outlines his course as follows: "In connection with the chair of Logic and Metaphysics, there are three courses of lectures delivered: logic and psychology in the junior class, and metaphysics, properly so called, in the advanced class" (October 29, 1880). The two courses serve as an introduction to the study of philosophy proper. "Philosophy professes that there is one central science—the science of sciences. Mind science is the portal of philosophy—i.e., the science of man." He defines logic as "the regulative science of thought," psychology as the science of the facts of consciousness, logic as the science of the forms and laws of thought, and philosophy as the craving for knowledge as viewed in its ultimate intellectual unity. He states that it is not by observation proper that man is to be studied but by reflection. It consists in making the mind its own object; it cannot be done by another; the student must perform the act himself.

These lectures are completely concerned with logic, and there is no mention of rhetoric or communication.

FRASER, ALEXANDER CAMPBELL. 1856–91. EUL MS Gen. 1902. 1 volume. Paginated. Handwriting small and difficult to read, ink faded, and binding good. *Lectures. Logic and Metaphysics. Prof. A. C. Fraser. Taken by C. F. Easterbrook* [name is unclear].

Logic is covered in pages 1–90; psychology in pages 91–184. The psychology lectures are dated and numbered. The manuscript contains an insert of smaller pages (43–48 and two unnumbered pages), but the lectures appear to be in sequence. The term *psychology* is used for the commonsense school in these lectures, which are heavily influenced by Hamilton. Rhetoric and communication are no longer a part of logic by the time of these course notes.

English Literature

GRIERSON, HERBERT J. C. Aberdeen: 1894–1915; Edinburgh: 1915–35. EUL MS Gen. 2096–97D. Course in English. 2 volumes. 72 lectures. No pagination. Handwriting fairly clear, but the notes contain many abbreviations, making them difficult to read. Ink somewhat faded, binding good. *English. Professor Grierson. Taken by Marie W. Stuart. 1916–17.*

These two volumes represent the notes of a course in a three-year sequence of courses in English between 1916 and

1919 taken by Marie W. Stuart during Grierson's first years at the University of Edinburgh immediately after he left the University of Aberdeen in 1915. The seventy-two lectures begin on October 13, 1916, and end on March 19, 1917. The school year usually extended into May; there is no explanation for this early termination.

This first set of lectures is titled "Rhetoric and Composition" at the beginning of lecture 1 with eight subheadings:

1. The Scope of Ancient Rhetoric
2. The Point of View in Composition and a Classification of Kinds of Style
3. Words
4. Figurative Language
5. The Sentence
6. The Paragraph
7. Composition Expository, Oratorical and Imaginative
8. Rhythm in Prose and Verse

These subheadings are followed by a short history of rhetoric, its revival in the Renaissance, and "in [the] nineteenth century in general [a] tendency to drop rhetoric." Rhetoric he defines not as the "art of composition, although we've dropped much of Aristotle. . . . a good deal survives in criticism—novel or play—not confined to style and construction." He points out that ancient rhetoric has been enlarged.

Each of the eight topics listed above is treated at intervals throughout the lectures on literature in lectures 1, 5, 9, 13, 17, 21, 25, and 31. Thus, eight lectures treat rhetoric and composition, while the remaining sixty-six treat literature. This set of notes is interspersed with notes from tutorials. There is one essay assignment, on the page opposite the first lecture, with the title "Qualities of Spenser's Poetry as Illustrated in Book IV of Faerie Queen."

It is interesting to note that this appears to be a set of notes rather than a script dictated by the professor as in the case of Masson's lecture notes. Incomplete sentences are interspersed with dashes and many abbreviations, particularly in the tutorials. For example, "Slight things before

16-copy-bks—scenes fr. tale—meant to be nonsensical—str. forward nervouse Eng.—naive-sprightliness-to 21-more def. satiric-v. existig conventions in fiction—burlesque & satire—improb. events-orig. nonsense. . . ."

GRIERSON, HERBERT J. C. Aberdeen: 1894–1915; Edinburgh: 1915–35. EUL MS Gen. 2098–2101D. 4 volumes. A total of 152 lectures in all, delivered between 1917 and 1919. No pagination. Handwriting fairly clear, but notes contain many abbreviations, making them difficult to read. Ink somewhat faded, binding good. 2098D: *English Language*. 1917–18. Professor Grierson. Taken by Marie W. Stuart. 2099D: *English Literature*. Professor Grierson. 1917–18. Taken by Marie Wilson Stuart. 2100D: *English Literature*. Sessions 1917–18 and 1918–19. Professor Grierson. Taken by M. M. W. Stuart. 2101D: *English Literature*. Session 1918–19. Professor Grierson. Taken by M. M. W. Stuart.

These volumes are the continuation of Miss Stuart's studies under Professor Grierson. Volume 1 (2098D), entitled *English Language*, contains forty-three lectures that extend from October 14 or 15 to May 28. The volume covers primarily Old English language and literature, with the last nine lectures covering the period of Middle English.

Volume 2 (2099D) starts with Chaucer and goes through the Elizabethan period, concluding with the minor dramatists. There are thirty-eight lectures, beginning October 9 and ending February 6.

Volume 3 (2100D) starts with lecture 39 on February 12 and then contains notes from a summer term in 1918 of eleven lectures that cover English prose from Bacon. Notes from the autumn session, which is concerned primarily with Shakespeare, begin on October 8, 1918, with lecture 1. The twenty-first lecture concludes the term on December 18, 1918.

Volume 4 (2101D) continues with the period 1660 to 1760, covering the second term from January 14, 1919, to May 30, with twenty-two lectures covering the poetry, novels, and drama of the period.

⅚ | 5

The University of Glasgow

The University of Glasgow was founded by William Turn-bull, a bishop of Glasgow who through James II petitioned the pope for the establishment of a university in that city. Following the democratic spirit of all the Scottish universities, fees were based on the ability to pay. The sons of the nobility and barons of Scotland paid the highest fees, "those of the second rank, who, though inferior to the Barons, possessed means sufficiently ample," were to pay slightly less, and the poor "were to be admitted free of all charge" (*Report,* 1831, 219). The order of instruction was strictly inscribed. "In the first class from the 1st of October to the 1st of March, the principles of Greek grammar were to be taught," and from March to September the "precepts of eloquence," with copious examples from Plato, Cicero, Demosthenes, Homer, Aristophanes, and Aristotle. In the second class, "the whole art of Rhetoric was to be amply treated"; in the third and fourth classes, arithmetic; geometry; Aristotle's logic, ethics, and politics; physics; the doctrine of the sphere; cosmography; introduction to universal history; and the principles of the Hebrew tongue were covered (*Report,* 1831, 219). The Royal Commissioners' *Report* describes the student's day.

> Five in the morning was to be the hour of rising; at six every Master was to enter his class-room and examine the Students, and otherwise instruct them till eight. The whole were then to proceed to public prayers, a duty which was not to occupy more than half an hour. From

94

prayers they were to retire separately to their private studies, and revise the morning exercises till nine; half an hour
was then to be allowed for breakfast, and study was to be
resumed till ten. (219)

And the day continued in this structured manner until nine P.M.
when the students were expected to be in bed. The rules governing
their conduct were equally strict.

> No one was to enter a tavern, or bowling-green, or to
> play at rackets or to play at all, except when leave was
> granted to all, and even then not be more than a quarter
> of an hour in the fields. . . . Any student attacking an-
> other to the effusion of blood was to be expelled . . . and
> anyone detected in nocturnal rambles, was to be punished
> with the greatest severity. (219)

Swimming was absolutely prohibited, and anyone indulging in
this sport was to be "beaten with many stripes and expelled" (219).
The life of the masters was equally regimented. The masters
were usually recent graduates of the college who were obliged
according to their degree requirements to teach for several years
while awaiting appointment to a parish. They accompanied their
students to and from the playing fields, and any master who
attacked another "to the effusion of blood" was not only expelled
but deprived of his degree. They were appointed by the modera-
tors of the university and were "bound to serve six years," a
condition that they seldom fulfilled. Each was also required to take
an oath not to marry and was compelled to forfeit his appointment
if he did so (*Report*, 1831, 220). With the regenting system still
in effect, each master took his students with him through all four
years teaching all subjects. The regents were generally young, and
competition for these positions was usually keen (Kerr 117).

In 1574, Andrew Melville returned from the Continent,
where he had been a professor at Geneva, and took over as principal
at Glasgow. Under the *Novo Erectio et Fundatio*, the regent, for the
first time in Scotland, was assigned to only one department, thus
introducing the beginning of the professorial system. It continued
until 1641, when regenting was reintroduced. In 1727, the profes-

sorial system was finally reestablished. After Melville's reforms, the university again went into a period of decline, and a lack of discipline and general rowdiness prevailed among students and masters at the end of the seventeenth century and the beginning of the eighteenth. "On many occasions during the next twenty years students were either expelled or severely censured for long absences from lectures, breaches of the peace, indecency, drinking in ale-houses with disreputable people, and scandalously irreverent behaviour in church" (Kerr 227). Instruction was still in Latin, a requirement that made courses difficult and irrelevant. A number of honest efforts were made to improve the situation, and with the appointment of Professor Francis Hutcheson to the chair of moral philosophy in 1728, lectures in Latin were gradually abandoned. Though many professors realized the futility of such lecturing, Hutcheson was the first to take a stand. "By lecturing in English . . . he stirred up intellectual life, invested his subject with fresh interest, and gave the first hearty impulse to the pursuit of philosophy in Scotland" (Kerr 231). Other professors soon followed. The salaries of the professors were small but they were augmented by student fees and by numerous fringe benefits, such as meals at the common table.

By the beginning of the eighteenth century, only forty of the nearly four hundred students "lived in," and the university ceased being a residential institution. The nineteenth-century students were allowed admission to the library on the payment of a small fee, according to an 1844 calendar, and for "academic purposes" were divided into *togati* (liberal arts students) and *non-togati*. As in all the Scottish universities, a liberal arts education was deemed an essential preliminary to professional education, so the togati students were generally younger "and subjected to a stricter discipline and more vigilant superintendence than the rest" (14). Their attendance at classes and examinations was compulsory. The togati included public and private students, but only the former were required to take examinations. The non-togati, having finished their liberal arts instruction, were studying in a profession. They also included "persons of maturer age who are residents in the city or its vicinity; and who, though engaged in other avocations, are still disposed to cultivate the literary pursuits of their earlier years, or to extend their acquaintance with some favourite branches of learning or science, by attending the lectures given at the University" (GUL Calendar, 1844, 15). An interesting example of the non-togati is represented in GUL Ms. Gen. 40/1–2, a particularly clear set of notes taken by James Ballantyne and donated to the library by his grandson as "an example of what interested at least one Glasgow businessman" in 1866.

During the nineteenth century, the University of Glasgow served a heterogeneous student body, made up of all ages, classes, and occupations. Centered in the thriving city, however, its curriculum was largely shaped to serve its particular constituency of merchants and their sons. These successful merchants believed in a liberal arts education, but they also believed in getting an early start in business. "A youth destined for business is not in the fair way of gaining success in life if, at the age of eighteen, he is still loitering over his books" (qtd. in R. D. Anderson, *Education* 78).

Nineteen new professorships were established in the nineteenth-century Scottish universities, including the chair of English language and literature at Glasgow in 1861. Logic and rhetoric were taught together within a single course by a series of distinguished Scotsmen: George Jardine, 1787; Robert Buchanan, 1827; John Veitch, 1864; Robert Adamson, 1895.

In 1858, largely due to the popularity of Professor Aytoun's course at Edinburgh, the Royal Commission decreed that English be added to the logic courses at all of the Scottish universities. This study of English included literature, history, and often a bit of geography. Three years later, the chair of English language and literature was founded at Glasgow by ordinance of the Royal Commissioners as a gift from the Crown. The first holder of the chair, John Nichol, was appointed in 1862 and held it until 1889.

George Jardine was named professor of logic and rhetoric in 1774, a position he held for nearly forty years. He had formerly been professor of Greek, and he moved with ease into his new chair. He was an outspoken champion of the Scottish system of education. During his long tenure, he was deeply involved in the major educational issues of the day: liberal arts versus specialization and instruction in the classics versus instruction in English. He also supported discussion and writing as a way of learning in conjunction with lectures, and, although his name is unfamiliar to us, his ideas are preserved in his students' notes and in his book,

Outlines of Philosophical Education, first published at the University Press of Glasgow in 1818 and reprinted in 1825.[1]

Jardine supported the idea on which the University of Glasgow was founded and regarded the arts not as vocational training but as preparation for later specialization. He recognized the differences between the English system of education and the Scottish one.

> So great indeed is the difference in the means and system of instruction adopted in the several universities of Great Britain, that it might, for a moment, appear doubtful, whether the minds to be cultivated were really of the same order, and the professional qualification to be attained had any thing in common. (415–16)

He argued that a plan of education should be formed "according to the state of knowledge, and the prevailing pursuits of the period in which it originates. . . . where the purpose of Greek education was to qualify young men to become 'good members of the commonwealth,' Roman education was to prepare youth 'for the business of the senate and of the bar' " (415–16). Education in the Middle Ages was to prepare candidates for service to the church, while Scottish education, according to Jardine, should be designed for "young men destined to fill various and very different situations in life," to allow them "to comprehend the elements of those other branches of knowledge, upon which the investigation of science, and the successful despatch of business are found chiefly to depend" (31). Jardine, however, knew that knowledge in itself was not enough and admonished his students: "A man may be capable of great reflections but if he cannot communicate it to others, it can be of but little use" (GUL Ms. Gen. 737, 2:155–56). He felt that writing and rhetoric in the fullest sense were central to the Scottish arts program.

Jardine also questioned the emphasis on Greek and Latin in the English universities: "We do not, in this part of the kingdom, attach to classical learning that high and almost exclusive degree of importance which is ascribed to it elsewhere" (418). According to Jardine, the practice of delivering the lectures of the first philosophy class in Latin was continued until 1750, "when Adam Smith was appointed professor of logic; and, being rather unexpectedly called to discharge the duties of his office, he found it necessary to read to his pupils, in the English language, a course of lectures on rhetoric and belles lettres, which he had formerly delivered in Edinburgh" (20). Adam Smith's successor followed his lead. English was established as the language of instruction by the middle of the nineteenth century.

The most important issue for Jardine, however, and of special interest today, concerned the lecture system of the Scottish universities. In *Outlines,* Jardine urged discussion sessions and regular writing exercises beyond the daily lecture. In this stand, he opposed not the English system, which was largely tutorial, but the prevailing practice at the other Scottish universities where most instruction was solely by lecture.

> It is with reluctance I repeat the remark, that, in several of our academical establishments, the philosophical education of youth is very imperfectly understood, and most inefficiently conducted. The exertion, whatever it may be, is almost entirely confined to the professor. The pupils are not required to do any thing. It is pretty much left to themselves whether they shall be utterly idle or practically employed, whether they shall derive any advantage from their attendance on the lecture, or go away, at the end of the course, as ignorant and uninformed as when it began. Surely, the common sense of the nation will not much longer permit such an abuse of the means of improvement. (523–24)

Jardine emphasized discussion hours, or the catechetical system, accompanied by theme writing in all classes. According to the statutes of the University of Glasgow, every professor, in addition to his morning lecture, was required to hold one class hour during the morning for the purpose of examining his students and assigning and hearing their writing exercises. Jardine kept his students for an additional hour each day in order that they might discuss the lectures and read or report on themes that had been assigned.

No one was more aware of the problems inherent in such a

system than Jardine, himself. He was the first to acknowledge that it imposed extra work for the professor and admitted that "this system of practical instruction is much more difficult than the composition of lectures" (293). He recognized that assigning a large number of themes was an added burden in classes that sometimes numbered two hundred students. He suggested, however, that the system was particularly necessary in the Scottish universities where there were many students "who are not qualified, either in respect of age or of previous acquirements" (427).

The problems encountered by Jardine sound familiar, and his solutions are enlightening for teachers of writing at the college level today who face large classes and inadequately prepared students. His lecture review through discussion and writing, his sequenced assignments, and his methods of theme writing and evaluation were designed not only to instruct students in basic writing but also to allow the professor to work with large numbers of written assignments.

During the first half of the examination period, the professor quizzed the students on the content of the lecture. The purpose of the questions, Jardine asserted, was to elicit from the students "the knowledge they have acquired by the lecture, expressed in their own manner." But he warned that "the same questions cannot be put indiscriminately." There may be some who have no trouble answering the question, but "there are many who, from inattention, defect of memory, or want of intellect . . . require that hints should be supplied to aid their recollection" (282). He added that the professor should proceed with "kindness and affability" with those students who "cannot overcome the embarrassment into which they are thrown by their natural timidity" (282). In citing the advantages of the discussion hour, Jardine concluded by advising the instructor that "he may frequently seize a favourable opportunity for rousing the indolent, for encouraging the diffident, for directing the spirit of the adventurous, and for bringing down the pretensions of the petulant and the assuming" (285).

During the second part of the discussion hour, Jardine instructed his students "to produce an abridgment in writing of all they have heard in the morning—the order, the method, the principal topics, and the illustrations—as far as they can recollect them" (287). After the students had finished this exercise, they were called on "indiscriminately and at random" to read portions of their writing. As an alternative to this writing exercise, a professor might ask a certain number of students to draw up an abridgment of the lecture while the others were engaged in discussion, allowing them to learn the art of "excluding the distracting influence of external objects" (288). Jardine asserted that this exercise combined different activities of the mind: "The students have to remember,—to select and arrange the materials furnished to them, and to express, on the spur of the occasion, their ideas in plain and perspicuous language" (289–90).

In his method of theme assignments, Jardine recognized the necessity of ordering the assignments in degree of difficulty as the session progressed. In the first order of themes, assigned during the first two months of the session, the topics were based on the lectures. These themes, assigned almost every day, were, in effect, short essays to be written at night and read in class the next day. The object for the student was "to form clearer and more accurate notions of the subjects discussed in the lectures than can be acquired from merely hearing them delivered," as well as accustoming the student "to express his thoughts on these subjects in correct and perspicuous language" (297).

In the second order of themes, the topics required the student "to cultivate the faculties, whose office it is to arrange and classify the subjects of our knowledge, according to their nature and relations" (303). Jardine gave examples of possible topics: "How may the books in a library be arranged, according to a natural or an artificial classification?" "In what way may the whole words of a language be brought under certain classes?" (305).

In the third order of themes, the student was required "to judge and reason for himself" (307). Jardine's lectures furnished full directions for the exercise of reason and judgment and were supplemented by readings. But he saw reason and communication closely allied. "The faculty of reason and of speech depend greatly on, and assist each other. It is the faculty of reasoning which leads us to use the faculty of communication, and the latter faculty which exists in improving the former. The faculty of reason and speech therefore have a reciprocal effect on each other" (GUL Ms. Gen. 737, 2:155–56). Suggested topics for third-order themes were "Is the institution of prizes in universities useful?" "Do holidays promote study?" "Whether is a town or a country life most favourable to study?" Jardine acknowledged that not all students would have sufficient knowledge to write about such subjects; however, he recognized the value of prewriting and drafts—the concept of writing as a process: "In all cases, perfect specimens must be preceded by many unsuccessful efforts." But these efforts are "the natural and indispensable steps which lead to higher degrees of perfection," especially when "properly submitted to a teacher, who can direct how they may be rendered more complete." Jardine offered, in this connection, a cogent bit of advice for student writers: "It is abundantly obvious, that if a young man did not begin to compose on any subject till he had obtained a complete knowledge of it, he would never begin at all, and the season of forming that important habit would be utterly lost" (313).

The object of the fourth and final order of themes was to lead the student "to improve those faculties of the mind which are employed in the higher processes of investigation" (322). Jardine demonstrated that these exercises were to improve "the powers of attention, discrimination, and investigation—to conduct the mind from phenomena to causes, from particular to general truths, and thus to produce habits of reasoning which may easily be applied to other subjects" (328). Finally, Jardine advised that, occasionally, students should be allowed to choose their own subjects for themes. "Rules prevent deviations and irregularities, but they can never create inventions, or lead to higher degrees of excellence," and, he added, "the noblest works of genius have not been the result of precept." Therefore, he urged that young persons should be allowed on occasion "to make bold attempts, to disdain the little limits of their reign" (352). He added, however, a precaution that students should be "required to subjoin a signed declaration to their theme, that it is their own composition, and not copied or altered from any author" (353). Jardine further warned that themes must be "prescribed frequently and regularly" and that the subjects also must be various and numerous.

> Were the same topics given out every succeeding session, there would be a great risk of idle and negligent students borrowing and copying those of a former year, and even attentive students might occasionally have recourse to

such performances to abridge their labour. In this case, themes, like the strings of syllogisms, formerly well known in some celebrated seminaries, would become a sort of college property, descending from one generation to another. (294)

In the matter of determining the merits of themes, Jardine devised a process designed not only to aid the student but also to alleviate some of the burden of the professor. He admitted that the time and labor required to examine the themes of a class might seem to be "considerable" but that "experience and habit [would] enable the teacher to execute this work more expeditiously than might at first sight be believed" (364). Jardine urged the instructor not to "give offence" in the exposure of defects, "a matter of considerable delicacy" (365). He acknowledged the difficulty of dealing with the treatment of the "more faulty exercises." "Were he to expose them in the unqualified terms of disapprobation which they may possibly deserve, he might ruin every chance of being useful to the authors." So he advised the instructor to overlook some of these first faults while "neglecting no opportunity of encouraging the student to do better" (366).

In dealing with the large number of themes in "so numerous a class," Jardine recognized that the instructor could not possibly examine all of the papers, and yet he also advised that, unless they were all regularly examined or "brought to public notice," the students whose exercises were overlooked would "become relaxed, their spirits depressed, and their feelings irritated. . . . If our essays pass without notice, they naturally ask, why need we give ourselves so much trouble in composing them?" (367). He suggested that the first class of themes be read aloud to the class, and the professor could at that time make appropriate remarks. Or, as an alternative, the professor could mark the papers at home and then read certain ones of them aloud the following day, commenting on general defects or merits.

For the second- and third-order themes, Jardine suggested the system of appointing ten or twelve of the best students to serve as examinators. However, he applied strict rules for these examinators. First, they were expressly prohibited from discussing the themes with other students. Second, they were to begin by

103

reading the whole theme in order to understand its general outline. Third, they were instructed not merely to point out defects but also to select those parts of the essay that deserved to be read in class. Fourth, the examinators were required to couch their criticisms in "liberal and becoming terms." Finally, the examinators, as well as all of the students in the class, were never to mention outside of the class any criticisms that had been made on the essays. A violation of any one of these rules would result in immediate dismissal from the class.

Recognizing the power and efficacy of peer evaluation and the merits of such a system, Jardine suggested "the idea of extending to every one, in his own turn, an opportunity for exercising his powers of criticism" (371). Finally, Jardine introduced into the arts curriculum the awarding of prizes for themes—the themes to be judged by fellow students. "It may be imagined, at first view, that the office of judge would best be performed by the professor; but, after long experience, and much attention to the subject in all its bearings, I am inclined to give a decided preference to the exercise of this right as vested in the students" (385).

This program, developed nearly 150 years ago by Professor George Jardine at the University of Glasgow, was ideal in serving the needs of a nation attempting to make access to education available to all citizens. It furnished a broad liberal arts education. Jardine and his colleagues saw a full rhetoric—the ability to reason, to investigate, to judge, to write, and to speak—as an integral part of that education. Although Jardine had never heard such phrases as *peer evaluation, writing as discovery, writing across the curriculum,* and *writing as process,* he was quite familiar with the concepts.

His course was popular, rising from fifty students to more than two hundred during his tenure. He was a strong advocate for the Scottish lecture system, as opposed to the English tutorial practice, as long as the lectures were followed by regular question-and-answer sessions in which the students discussed the lectures, polished their notes (which they later copied), and wrote themes (which were read aloud). Jardine's *Outlines* is a valuable source in investigating his philosophy of teaching and gives insight into Scottish university education at its best.

Robert Buchanan served as Jardine's assistant until the latter's death in 1827; again, this was a common custom at the time. In his testimony before the Royal Commission in 1827, Buchanan still had not received his appointment, a fact that he made clear to the examiners by repeating over and over that he "was not yet a member of the faculty" (*Evidence, Glasgow* 36). Although he was highly respected and considered an authority on Scottish philosophy, the *Dictionary of National Biography* calls him "averse to independent and original speculations." He was educated as a minister and held the chair of logic and rhetoric for thirty-seven years. He was, in addition, a prolific writer, like many of his colleagues, and published numerous treatises on public issues. He also wrote poetry and drama connected with Scottish history.

We have an ample description of the way in which Buchanan conducted his course from his evidence before the Royal Commissioners (*Evidence, Glasgow* 35–43, 183–86). He asserted that he had continued to conduct his class as Professor Jardine had done except for slight modifications of his own. From 8:30 to 9:30 A.M., he lectured to his students in the logic class. At eleven o'clock, the students met again to be examined on the material in the lecture and to read their assigned essays. During this hour, he criticized the essays; and toward the end of the session, when the essays were longer—thirty to forty pages—he took them home, examined them carefully, and reported on them in class. "The shorter essays are read by the students themselves, in their places, and I criticise them as they are read" (37). He described his course in logic as consisting of three parts. In the first part, he covered the "analysis of the intellectual powers, or the elements of pneumatology"; the second part he called "logic proper"; and the third he described as "the art of communicating our thoughts, judgments, and reasonings, not only with precision, and perspicuity, but with elegance and force—the first being necessary for the Logician—the second for the Rhetorician" (37). His class included both logic and rhetoric. He asserted that his class met five days a week for two, sometimes three hours, and for one hour on Saturday. He considered the catechetical examination and the hearing of essays to be the most important part of his course. He followed Jardine's lead in awarding prizes and allowed the students to be the sole judges, insisting that he had seldom found their decisions to be different from his own. He also added in his testimony before the Royal Commission that, as a part of the final lecture, he assigned reading for the vacation.

Buchanan, disagreeing with Jardine, defended the teaching of Latin and Greek, asserting that "the knowledge of Greek and Latin is indispensably necessary, not merely for the scholar, but for the accomplished gentleman." He admitted, however, that every year, he received "numerous applications for enrollment in Logic class that I am obliged to refuse, because the applicants will not undertake to stand the Greek examination" (185). He described a conversation that he had had with the father of two young sons in Glasgow. The father observed:

> I would have sent those boys to College; but, according to the present system, they must spend three or four years upon Greek and Latin, in order to get at the other classes, and all the time I could afford to give them at College would thus be spent on the very branches which will be of least use to them in those mercantile pursuits for which I intend them. (Qtd. in *Evidence, Glasgow* 185)

The Royal Commissioners sympathized with this father's viewpoint, when one of them commented that the result of the insistence on Latin and Greek would be "to debar from the benefit of University education, and from instruction in science and philosophy, a great portion of the community of Glasgow, who would otherwise have had the benefit of it" (184). Buchanan agreed. The University of Glasgow took very seriously its commitment to the citizens of the city—largely members of the mercantile class. When they later opposed the strict entrance examinations, they did so on the basis of this strong commitment to the community.

John Veitch, the third nineteenth-century holder of the chair, studied at the University of Edinburgh with Professor Aytoun and with Professor William Hamilton, whom he later assisted at Edinburgh in the chair of logic and metaphysics. Veitch was elected to the chair of logic, rhetoric, and metaphysics at the University of St. Andrews, where he was required by mandate of the commission to include English literature in his course. From this study evolved his lifelong interest in Scottish poetry, out of which grew the writings for which he is best remembered. He was appointed to the chair of logic and rhetoric at Glasgow in 1864 and held the position for thirty years. The *Dictionary of National Biography* makes the following cryptic statement about his teaching:

> As a thinker Veitch was at odds with the chief movements of his day, and by adopting an extreme, and often contemptuous attitude of criticism, he balked himself of formative influence with the thousands of students who came under his care. Those of them who knew him intimately were affected by his personal character, not by his prelections. (20:200)[2]

We have only one set of notes from Veitch, but this set is full and developed. His lectures differ markedly from those of Jardine and Buchanan, but they were delivered after the chair of English literature was established in 1861. His course contains four sections on philosophy, psychology, logic, and rhetoric, the last receiving full and comprehensive treatment. He presents his own definition of rhetoric as the "doctrine or theory of literary composition" and includes both prose and poetry. He equates it with the term *literary criticism,* which he defines as "the science of analysis." He includes among types of "literature" a long section on historical writings.

The final holder of the chair in the nineteenth century, Robert Adamson, studied at the University of Edinburgh with Professors Aytoun and Hamilton and acted as assistant to the chairs of moral philosophy and logic and metaphysics at Edinburgh. He was later appointed professor of philosophy and political economy at Owens College at Manchester before he was elected to the chair at Glasgow. Like most of the professors of the time, he moved with ease from one discipline to another and from one university to another. He too was a prolific writer, active in the academic business of his day, and he was a strong supporter of admitting women students to degrees on equal terms with men. His course, again, was very different from those of his predecessors and more closely fit its title. Rhetoric was entirely excluded, although it is interesting to note that he included the newly important study of psychology within his course. At this time Alexander Bain at the University of Aberdeen was developing his popular course in psychology under the rhetoric rubric.

John Nichol, the first holder of the newly established chair of English language and literature at Glasgow, is best remembered as a poet and biographer. He is called "a brilliant and discontented teacher" in his biographical sketch in *British Authors of the Nineteenth Century* (471). His ideas on education and his views on literature and criticism are clearly set forth in his lectures, and his small volume, *English Composition*, gives his ideas on composition, which he clearly considered his responsibility.

Nichol's inaugural lecture, delivered in 1862 when he assumed the chair of English literature, clearly expresses his rather traditional views. His idea that the study of literature embodied a moral and nationalistic vision is a common sentiment for his time. In the lecture delivered in 1891 after his retirement, he defended the concept of taste and asserted that the idea that there is no standard of taste is "fatal to the hope of genuine instruction in any art" (GUL Y 1-i25.21). His small book on English composition (GUL ENG D 408 NIC) has lost all connection with a full rhetoric and, with the exception of the small section on versification, sounds very much like the composition textbooks of the same period in the United States. It is entirely prescriptive and filled with phrases like "correct grammar," "rules," and "laws that bind or ought to bind us."

The nineteenth-century University of Glasgow was designed to serve the citizens of that city. It was an open university in much the same sense that the City University of New York has been in the twentieth century. The professors in the chair of logic and rhetoric held their positions for years; and Jardine's methods prefigure many of the pedagogical theories of modern composition specialists. Unfortunately, his ideas did not prevail after the reforms in the latter part of the century. Nichol brought to the newly established chair of English literature many of the ideas gleaned from the rhetoric course, and he, more than any of the earlier professors of rhetoric, saw English composition in the reductive sense that it was to assume for many years in the universities of the United States.

The University of Glasgow: Archival Materials

The chair of logic and rhetoric was held by four professors. George Jardine, whose teaching methods we know primarily through his book, *Outlines of Philosophical Education*, held the position for thirty years. He was followed by George Buchanan and John Veitch, who each occupied the chair for over thirty years, and finally by Robert Adamson. In 1861, near the end of Buchanan's tenure, the chair of English language and literature was established. John Veitch was its first holder. In the citations that follow, the professor's name and the years of his professorship are followed by the library in which the manuscript is located, its call number, and any pertinent information about its condition, such as legibility, number of pages, if it is paginated or volumes. Libraries are abbreviated as follows: EUL, University of Edinburgh Library; GUL, University of Glasgow Library; AUL, University of Aberdeen Library; NLS, National Library of Scotland. The exact inscription on the title page then follows in italics. The manuscripts are listed in chronological order under the course title within which they were taught.

Logic and Rhetoric

JARDINE, GEORGE. 1787–1824. GUL MS Gen. 166. 263 pages. Handwriting clear, but ink faded, and binding bad. Title page and last page of index are missing. On page 55, it is dated December 10, 1782, and on page 140, January 29, 1783.

Although John Clow was the official holder of the chair of logic and rhetoric at this time, Jardine had been appointed professor of Greek and assistant to the professor of logic in 1774. He did not receive official appointment until 1787, a common occurrence in the Scottish universities of the period. Because of the similarity to the synopses of Jardine (GUL BG 44-i.10; GUL BC 28-H.3) and to the other set of Jardine's students' notes (GUL MS Gen. 737), these are probably notes from Jardine's early lectures rather than those of John Clow.

The notes are divided into three parts: logic, or, as Jardine would term it, the powers of knowledge, of which the first page is missing; the powers of taste (140); and the powers of communication (187).

The material is much the same as that included in the synopsis of 1813 (GUL BC 28-H.3) but under different headings. The third division contains the section on words,

109

sentences, and style, which includes the figures of speech, concluding with a short section on the kinds of composition. The notes conclude with the section on history, which is exactly like the one in the 1813 synopsis.

Jardine, George. 1787–1824. GUL MS Gen. 737/1–2. 2 volumes. Paginated separately: 737/1, 178 pp.; 737/2, 154 pp. Handwriting clear, but ink faded; binding good. *Notes taken by George Palmes at the College of Glasgow from the lectures of Mr. Jardine Professor of Logic. 1793/4.*

These notes, taken by a student early in Jardine's tenure of the chair of logic and rhetoric, predate the synopses published in 1797 and 1813. They do, however, follow the tripartite division customary in all of his lectures: metaphysics or practical logic, taste, and communication.

There is an interesting introductory section on the rules to be applied to themes and discourses (1:1–27). Jardine remarks that rules "have been laid down how to judge and reason, now it becomes necesssary to observe the application of them" (1:1). There follows an interesting discussion of a theme and a thesis. A theme in a logical sense is a subject proposed to be investigated. It is derived from anything "placed before the mind to enquire into, and to illustrate, or it may be something to prove or inforce" (1:1).

Themes are then divided into two types: simple and complex. The simple theme is expressed in one term, and its object is to explain it so that all who hear it may form clear notions of it (1:1). He gives four rules for the manner of handling the simple theme:

1. Explain the origin and meaning of the term.
2. Explain the essential qualities of the subject.
3. Consider its parts.
4. Consider its relation to other things.

Jardine then divides complex themes—those that treat "important and doubtful propositions" (1:8)—into two types: solitary and social. Thus, a theme "may be solitary . . . when the whole is performed by any individual, or it may be social

. . . when other persons bear a share in it" (1:7). He briefly discusses the parts of a theme with the introduction and with summing "up the whole at last" (1:12). But these, he tells us, will be "considered at the rhetorical hour" (1:12). He then considers a kind of social theme called a *dispute* and asserts that "the proposition which is used in this dispute is called a thesis" (1:22). He gives as one of the advantages of a disputation that it "brings out activity of minds which other modes of Education do not" (1:27) but warns that such "wrangling might be extended to every subject in common life" and thus has a tendency to "bring forward petulant characters" and "a turn of mind that would contradict everything" (1:27).

This discussion is a curious and enlightening blend of classical ideas and modern terminology, and certainly this concept of the terms *theme* and *thesis* has persisted in composition courses well into the twentieth century.

Jardine further demonstrates his modernity in his introduction to the third section, on communication, insisting on what modern composition theorists would call *recursiveness*. He maintains that the powers of communication depend greatly on the powers of acquiring knowledge and the powers of taste. The faculties of reason and speech depend greatly on and assist each other. It is the faculty of reasoning that leads us to use the faculty of communication, and the latter faculty assists in improving the former. The faculties of reason and speech therefore have a reciprocal effect on each other (1:155).

The sections on taste and communication follow Jardine's usual scheme, although the section on language, words, sentences, and style is here treated under communication and not under taste as it is in the 1813 synopsis or under the first and third divisions as it was in the 1797 synopsis. The communication division concludes with a long discourse on the three kinds of composition, classified according to the purpose of each: to instruct, to prove, or to excite the emotions. He then devotes sixty-five pages to a description of historical writings (2:93–120) and poetical compositions (2:120–54).

111

JARDINE, GEORGE. 1787–1824. GUL BG 44-i.10. 96 printed pages with two pages added in handwriting entitled "III: General Division On Taste." Also added in print, "*Quaedam ex Logicae Compendiis Selecta.* In Usum Studiosorum Class. Log. Glasguae: In AEdibus Academicis, Excudebat Jacobus Mundell, Academiae Typographus." 1797. 32 pages. Printing clear, binding very poor. *Synopsis of Lectures on Logic and Belles Lettres; Read in the University of Glasgow.* Glasgow: At the University Press, Printed by James Mundell, University Printer, 1797.

This short volume, printed by Jardine for his students, outlines the course for the year 1797. Jardine states as the object of the course "to explain the proper method of improving the faculties of reason, of taste, and of communication by speech and writing" (1). He divides the course into four parts.

> The first division will comprehend, an analysis of the faculties of the mind, chiefly those of the understanding—illustrated by the principles of language and of general grammar. The second division will comprehend, the art of improving those faculties of the mind, by which a knowledge of the causes, properties, and relations of things is acquired, illustrated by the history of logic and an explanation of the principal rules of that art. The third division will comprehend the art of improving the powers of taste, illustrated by the history of eloquence and of rhetoric. The fourth division will comprehend the art of improving the faculty of communication, illustrated by the history of eloquence and of rhetoric. (5–6)

Jardine then comments that the "first of these general divisions will serve as a foundation for the three which follow it" (6). Unfortunately, this small book only covers the first two divisions with a two-page appendage in handwriting on the third division.

The first division is a summary of the philosophy of common sense, concluding with a section on grammar, called "universal grammar," and a short section on arrangement. The second division is largely a history of logic, which Jardine divides into three periods. In the discussion of Aristotle, Jardine calls the syllogism a "useless instrument in the search of truth," maintaining that it "is of little use in extending the bounds of science" since it "is contrary to the natural process of investigation" (86). The third period in the history of logic, "the restoration of true learning" (90), he attributes to Ramus and Descartes and other foreign philosophers but primarily to Lord Bacon's *De Augmentis Scientiarum* and *Novum Organum*. The criticism of the syllogism derives from Bacon's works, and its applications to science and art derive from the same source.

Jardine concludes with the following commentary on the teaching of logic in the Scottish universities:

> The end and objects of the art of reasoning have of late been greatly promoted, by an alteration in the manner of teaching it, adopted in the universities of this country. Formerly the business of a first philosophy class was confined to an explanation of the logic and metaphysics of Aristotle. This was an improper introduction to the study of philosophy—and chiefly calculated to excite prejudices against logic. (95)

This is an interesting synopsis of Jardine's lectures because of its clear presentation of commonsense philosophy and the heavy influence of Thomas Reid, who was professor of moral philosophy at the University of Glasgow from 1764 to 1796. This small publication was obviously meant to supplement the lectures (see GUL MS Gen. 737 and GUL MS Gen. 166). It is written in topical form, and the words *illustration* and *example* are inserted at frequent intervals in places where the lecture clearly enlarged on a point in the synopsis.

JARDINE, GEORGE. 1787–1824. GUL BC 28-h.3. 84 pages with selections from Aristotle appended. Printing clear, but binding fragile. *Synopsis of Lectures on Logic and Belles Lettres: Read in the University of Glasgow*. Glasgow: Printed by Andrew Duncan, Printer to the University, 1813.

113

This second synopsis of lectures, printed sixteen years after the 1797 synopsis (GUL BG 44-i.10), is an update of Jardine's lectures and is markedly different. The course now consists of three parts, with part 1 including the first two divisions of the earlier synopsis. This course now includes the following parts:

Part 1: The improvement of the powers or faculties of knowledge
Part 2: The improvement of the powers of taste
Part 3: The improvement of the powers of communication.
. . . illustrated by the principles of eloquence and rhetoric

The first part is similar to the first two divisions in the earlier synopsis, but whereas that version had no printed synopsis on the division of taste, this version has forty-three pages (41–84).

The section on taste is divided into two sections: an analysis of the powers of taste, and the art or method of improving them. Jardine points out that taste was not a subject treated either by the Greek or Roman writers or by the scholastic philosophers. It is derived from French and English writers since "the revival of literature." "The sixth volume of the *Spectator*, contains the first regular analysis of the powers of Taste in the English language.—Mr. Addison has been followed by Hutcheson, Hume, Kames, Burke, Gerard, Blair, Alison, etc." (41). What follows is a complete analysis of the concept of taste as it was understood in the nineteenth century. The lectures on the improvement of taste (57) comprise a short introductory section on the origin of language, words, sentences, and style in outline form— presumably greatly enlarged in the lectures themselves. Jardine then divides compositions according to the "different ends that the composer has in view: to inform or instruct; to produce assent—belief, conviction; to excite emotions, affections, passions for the purpose of persuasion, or of pleasure and amusement" (61).

According to this division, compositions are divided

into three categories: historical, philosophical, or rhetorical. Jardine includes poetry under the rhetorical classification. He then discusses each of these categories, devoting the most space to poetical composition (66–82). He concludes this section with a short explanation of the rules for the art of criticism.

> The rules of the ancient critics were followed implicitly till the restoration of literature. After this period, critics arose, who looked beyond the ancient rules—to the nature of man—his capacities of receiving pleasure—to the general principles of the arts—and the end which the artists have in view—to the means by which that end may be best effected. . . . The office of the critic is not to praise or to censure—but to discover what deserves praise or censure. (83)

Unfortunately, part 3, "On the Powers of Communication," is missing and points to another synopsis that I have not been able to locate. The synopsis concludes with a cryptic note, "See Synopsis of Rhetoric" (84).

The student who owned this volume had an artistic bent, which finds expression in the margins of the book with men engaged in battle and street scenes of Glasgow. He also wrote in the author for the selections appended to the synopsis as the "Rev. J. G. Aristotle."

BUCHANAN, ROBERT. 1827–64. GUL MS Gen. 700. 561 pages. Except for an index and certain headings, these notes are in phonetic spelling and shorthand. *Nots ov Lecturz deliverd bi Robert Bucanan. M.A. Profesur ov Logic and Retoric in the Universiti ov Glasgo. Tacen during the sesun 1848–9 by Argibald Gardner.*

These notes, although not furthering our knowledge of Professor Buchanan's course in logic and rhetoric, are interesting because they demonstrate a popular movement in the nineteenth century toward phonetic spelling, a cause clearly espoused by this student.

115

BUCHANAN, ROBERT. 1827–64. EUL MS Gen. 636. 174 pages. 36 lectures. Paginated with good index. Handwriting readable, ink faded, and binding fragile. *Notes of the Lectures of R. Buchanan, Professor of Logic and Rhetoric. Session 1850–51. November 4th 1850. R. Flint. Glasgow.*

A quotation on the back of the title page, in handwriting different from the notetaker's reads,

The term *logic* (as also dialectic) is of ambiguous derivation. It may either be derived from [unclear], reason, or our intellectual faculties in general; or from [unclear], speech or language, by which these are expressed. The science of logic may, in like manner, be viewed either:—1; as adequately and essentially conversant-about-the former (the internal [unclear], verbum mentale,) and partially and accidentally about the latter, (the external [unclear] verbum oris;) or, 2; as adequately and essentially conversant-about-the latter, (the external [unclear]), partially and [unclear] accidentally about the former. Ham. Dis. p. 137. ratio. oratio.

In the "Introductory Lecture," Buchanan defines logic etymologically by definition (pointing out its essential qualities) and by comparison. In definition, he classifies it according to "those who extend its province the most, those who restrict it the most and those who hold a middle place" (2). The first definition "adopted by almost all the writers of the seventeenth century" (2) would include the "intellectual powers in our enquiries after truth and in communicating it to others" (2). It comes from those who include "method in their definition which properly comprehends Grammar and Rhetoric" (3).

Lectures 1, 2, and 3 define logic and reasoning. In lectures 4 and 5, he explains that logic is both an art and a science and outlines terms connected with logic that will be explained: substance, quality; mind, matter; powers, faculties; habits, instincts; cause, effect; idea, notion; sensation, perception; science, art; hypothesis, theory; analysis, synthesis. He covers these terms in the first six lectures. In lectures

7–10, he discusses the opposing theories of Descartes and Locke. Following Locke, lectures 11–14 discuss the senses, and lectures 16–20 discuss associationism and the law of transferences. In lectures 21 and 22, Buchanan discusses dreams; in 23, memory; in 24, volition; and in 25, judgment. The remaining lectures cover what the act of reasoning implies with attention to absence of mind and attention, abstraction and generalization, metaphorical language and imagination.

Buchanan explains that it is "the practice in this University to assign both Logic and Rhetoric to one chair. . . . The method in which we will treat Rhetoric will be explained when we have reached that length" (20). In the definition of logic, he compares it to rhetoric saying, "But something more than Logic is required. As social beings we require to exchange our thoughts for a variety of purposes. Their [sic] is an intimate connection between logic and rhetoric. From thinking and reasoning well, the transition is natural to communicating well" (21). In spite of his promise, Buchanan never gets to rhetoric in this set of thirty-six lectures. They may well represent only part of the full course.

BUCHANAN, ROBERT. 1827–64. NLS MS 8958. Pages numbered 271 to 302. Handwriting small, ink faded. Manner of binding makes reading difficult. *Notes on Logic (and Rhetoric) being the substance of Professor Buchanan's Lectures, as reported by I. Lang.*

These lecture notes are contained in a large volume of the papers (mostly letters) of S. Hislop, taken by Hislop. Starting with a definition of logic similar to the one outlined in EUL MS Gen. 636, Buchanan moves on to outline the three general divisions of the course.

  I. A short analysis and classification of the Intellectual powers which are thinking, judging and reasoning.
 II. Logic proper either as act or science—nature and laws of the Reasoning powers and an exposition of the Aristotelian Logic and the doctrine of Evidence.
III. The art of communicating our thoughts, judgments and Reasonings to others through speech or writing with

clearness, propriety and force—the philosophy of Taste and Rhetoric. (271 v)

Buchanan then notes that the first division involves reasoning powers while the second involves reasoning process. The first part of the course follows very closely the course notes taken by R. Flint in EUL MS Gen. 636 but takes up where those notes end, with the second part of the course "Logic Proper" (280). This section of the course is a rather straightforward description of Aristotelian logic, including the doctrine of predicaments or categories, definition, logical division, and the syllogism and "modern or Inductive logic" from Ramus, Bacon, Kames, and Campbell.

The third part of the course that concerns rhetoric is covered rather cursorily in only four pages. Rhetoric is defined as "the way to communicate our thoughts, judgments, and reasonings, with effect" (300). "Without a knowledge of the three sister arts, we cannot be good speakers" (300). As an art, it may be said to embrace two great branches— the philosophy of taste and the art of criticism—"those forms of it with which Rhetoric has specifically to do" (300).

The remainder of this brief section is a detailed discussion of the concept of taste as seen in nineteenth-century thought. The history of the term is traced from Baron Montesquieu to Edmund Burke and is finally defined by Buchanan as the complex capacity "of our rational and sensitive nature by which we experience those pleasures excited by the contemplation of the beautiful" (300).

BUCHANAN, ROBERT. 1827–64. GUL MS Gen. 661–62. Volume 1 is missing; volume 2: 418 pp.; vol. 3: 403 pp. with index. Dated November 24, 1859, to January 11, 1860. *Taken by David Murray.*

Although not officially listed as notes from the lectures of Buchanan's logic class, these notes are so similar to other students' notes from his class (NLS MS 8958; EUL MS Gen. 636) that there can be little doubt. In addition, the date puts them toward the end of his forty-year tenure as chair of logic and rhetoric.

Volume 2, directly following the consideration of the

five senses, goes over the familiar ground of his other lectures, covering in turn the association of ideas, the law of transference, a long section on the philosophy of dreams, and another on memory (327–29). He concludes the volume with a consideration of will and volition.

Volume 3 covers judgment, abstraction, imagination, and a history of logic (219). It concludes with a section called "Logic Proper," which outlines the principles of the syllogism and Bacon's inductive reasoning.

VEITCH, JOHN. 1864–95. GUL MS Gen. 40/1–2. 2 volumes paginated consecutively, 769 pp. Detailed index at beginning of vol. 1. Handwriting large and clear, binding good. *Notes of Lectures on Philosophy, Psychology, Logic and Rhetoric. Delivered by Professor Veitch in the Glasgow University. Session 1866–67.*

There is a letter bound in with this volume from J. B. Wood, who donated this set of notes to the University of Glasgow Library. He explains that the notes were taken by his grandfather, James Ballantyne, who was "in business in Glasgow as a jeweller." Wood writes that, although he is aware "that the subjects mentioned have undergone considerable modification since the time of Professor Veitch," he offers them nevertheless as "an example of what interested at least one Glasgow businessman in days when leisure was much more rare than it is now."

The index, outlining the contents of the course, is divided into the four parts mentioned on the title page: philosophy (1–89); psychology (89–422); logic (422–599); and rhetoric (599–769). It is interesting to note that these lectures were presented in 1866, five years after the establishment of the chair of English literature, which was at this time occupied by John Nichol (see GUL MS Gen. 277). Rhetoric, in this set of lectures, has become "literary criticism." These lectures are notably different from those of Veitch's predecessor in the chair, Professor Buchanan, who concentrated on logic and, as far as his students' notes and writings indicate, gave little or no attention to rhetoric.

Veitch's treatment of philosophy is sketchy and in only eighty-nine pages covers its general character, its relation to science, and the science of perception and reflection. Veitch then divides philosophy into three departments: psychology, logic, and metaphysics. He defines the science of psychology as "the inductive philosophy of the human mind. . . . the science of man . . . as a being capable of knowledge, feeling, desire and will" (30).

There is a lengthy, detailed section on psychology, which discusses, in order, knowledge, feeling, desire, and will. Knowledge embraces such subjects as memory and imagination and the existence or nonexistence of a material world outside of the mind. The section concludes with the familiar discussion of external perception through the senses: sensation and perception as modes of building up knowledge of the external world.

At the beginning of the section on logic, Veitch maintains that logic is the science of thought, not of expression—in sharp contrast to the ideas of many of his predecessors. He does, however, admit the close relationship when he says that "the use of language indicates a certain degree of mental development and that it also aids this development" (512).

The section on rhetoric, covering more than 150 pages, is one of the fullest treatments we have of the subject at this time. Veitch begins with a discussion of the interconnections between psychology and logic; thus, the principal point of rhetoric, "that which is expressed in language," is based in those subjects (599). It is interesting that he reviews the popular notions of rhetoric as the art of decorating a discourse in a certain gaudy and obtrusive ornamentation (601) and "that it is an art, the prevailing purpose of which is to deceive by means of specious but ill founded arguments—as a means of sophistry, circumvention and deceit" (602). He calls these views "vulgar errors—the hasty views of either an uneducated or an unreflective mind" (602). After reviewing Aristotle's definition, he presents his own.

By rhetoric, I mean the doctrine or theory of literary composition whether in prose or poetry and whatever be its end. Rhetoric as thus used is equivalent to the phrase literary criticism. Rhetoric enquires into the principle which regulates composition. Literary criticism is therefore viewed in the first instance as the science of analysis—the matter which it analyzes is literary composition. (604–5)

In criticism, Veitch continues, the mind "reflects on what it reads, to examine, to enquire, and scrutinize" (605). He then considers composition in two ways: first, according to its end or aim, and second, according to the character of the thoughts or ideas suitable to our end or purpose (610). These two points will determine the kinds of composition. He then reviews the character of literature and its influence and introduces narration and description, describing them with copious examples from Wordsworth, Shakespeare, and Milton. He devotes a long section to history—a form of writing that occupied the attention of many of these professors—and concludes with a section on style that includes diction and syntax, as well as a short history of language and discussion of the dictionary.

This section on rhetoric is interesting for its completeness and for the fact that it was being taught as something apart from English literature (which, again, was being taught at that time by Professor Nichol). Veitch views rhetoric and literary criticism as being one and the same.

ADAMSON, ROBERT. 1895–1902. GUL MS Gen. 281. 278 pages. Handwriting small and very difficult to read, but clear marginal notes helpful. Paginated. Beginning of an index is on the back of the title page. Ink clear, binding weak. *Logic by Robert Adamson. 1898–99. Psychology, Theory of Knowledge?* [sic] *taken by Archie D. Thomson.*

This set of notes from Professor Adamson's lectures is one of three sets taken in three successive years by Archie D. Thomson. Another set is dated 1900–1901 (GUL MS Gen. 283), and a third set was taken the following year, 1901–2 (GUL MS Gen. 282). Both of these later sets are entitled "Honours Logic."

In his introductory lecture, Adamson begins with a discussion of error, which he defines as basically "misapprehen-

121

sion" (3). Thus, he maintains that "the treatment of error" presses upon us three problems or areas of study (5):

1. The Logical Problem: the attempt to lay out systematically the conditions and methods of valid thinking, i.e., knowledge.
2. The Psychological Problem: the attempt to determine what is the character and what are the real conditions of the process whereby knowledge becomes actual in our thinking.
3. The Metaphysical Problem: the assumption on which logic proceeds—that it is possible for human thinking to reach "Truth." (5)

Adamson then presents a general theory of knowledge from three points of view: logical, psychological, and metaphysical. In the next lecture, he defines theoretical philosophy as "the consideration of knowledge in all its aspects as dealing with knowledge exclusively."

Adamson then moves to a consideration of Aristotelian logic followed by formal logic, which he calls an activity wholly separated from the matter of knowledge and which operates according to laws peculiar to itself. It therefore represents "a constant unchanging element in our organized knowledge" (64). It appears to be a fairly regular treatment of Aristotelian logic with some influence from Bacon.

The second division of the course, psychology, begins with lecture 47 (113). Adamson points out differences between knowing, feeling, and willing. He refutes faculty psychology and concentrates on associationism (127) and other contemporary nineteenth-century theories, such as George Berkeley's theory of vision (176).

These notes are complex and difficult to impossible to read. Under such circumstances, I have represented them as accurately as possible.

ADAMSON, ROBERT. 1895–1902. GUL MS Gen. 283. Neither lectures nor pages are numbered. Handwriting small and difficult to read, but clear marginal notes helpful. Ink clear, binding weak. *Adamson—Early Greek Philosophy especially Plato. Session 1900–1901. Honours Logic taken by Archie D. Thomson.* A comment on the title page reads as follows:

> With lectures on Kant and (starting from the other end—Psychology (analytical, I think)). These lectures are full, practically not a word lost. Prof. Adamson lectured without paper, only a book or two (Greek, French, German, English) in front of him with a slip of paper inside to open at the passage he wanted read (which passage he translated, if not in English, there and then *without reading aloud first the original language)*. What is placed in brackets are explanatory remarks he added by the way.

These notes may in fact be a word-for-word account of Professor Adamson's lectures, but the difficulty of making out what they say because of the handwriting negates their value. It would take a great deal of patience to sort out what is important and what is not important. Working largely from the marginal notes, I can make only the following very general comments.

The first section of these lectures is a review of the history of philosophy. The second section, "Psychology," is introduced with the following statement: "Psychology, at present, [is] at once the most progressive of the branches of philosophy, that which attracts most of the workers in the philosophy field and the subject in which the general principles and methods are most of all [a] matter of debate." (There is no page number; it is the first page of the reverse side of the original notes.) Adamson states that the common aim of psychology has been to eliminate erroneous vices and concepts. It is interesting to trace the increasing interest in psychology throughout these nineteenth-century lectures on logic and rhetoric and to see here that it is beginning to assert itself as a separate subject as evinced in this opening remark.

ADAMSON, ROBERT. 1895–1902. GUL MS Gen. 282. No page numbers. Handwriting small and difficult to read because all of these notes are in pencil. Good marginal notes in the second part of the lectures, entitled "Kant: Development from the Empirical Side." Binding strong. *Honours Logic: 1901–1902. Prof. R. Adamson's Lectures on Aristotle and Kant (development from Empirical Side). Taken by A. D. Thomson.*

Again, see also two other sets of lecture notes by Archie D. Thomson on Adamson's lectures (GUL MS Gen. 281; GUL MS Gen. 283). A note on the title page written in Thomson's difficult handwriting reads: "Prof. Adamson's Last Honours Class Lectures (every word of them practically). These lectures are a fragment as Prof. A. dies in the middle of them." I did not try to decipher these notes, except to ascertain that the subjects covered are pretty much those indicated on the title page.

ADAMSON, ROBERT. 1895–1902. *The Development of Modern Philosophy with Other Lectures and Essays,* ed. W. R. Sorley (Prof. in the University of Cambridge). Edinburgh and London: William Blackwood and Sons, 1903. 2 volumes: vol. 1, 358 pp.; vol. 2, 315 pp. GUL Phil BN 20 ADA2.

These two volumes are the published lectures of Robert Adamson. The first volume covers modern philosophy from Descartes through empiricism, with heavy emphasis on Kantian theories, concluding with a section on a theory of knowledge. The second volume covers psychology, with emphasis on theories of thinking. This is a full, clear, easily read presentation of Adamson's lectures published the year after his death. He was a widely published writer and lecturer whose own theories never crystallized and who is only of historical interest now in the newly emerging courses in psychology still included under logic and rhetoric.

ADAMSON, ROBERT. 1895–1902. *A Short History of Logic,* ed. W. R. Sorley (Prof. in the University of Cambridge). Edinburgh and London: William Blackwood and Sons, 1911. 262 pages. GUL E4-f.10.

Edited by W. R. Sorley, a professor at Cambridge and a fellow of the British Academy, this is a longer version of the article on logic that Adamson contributed to the ninth edition of the *Encyclopaedia Britannica.* According to Sorley, the editor of the *Encyclopaedia* "struck out a number of passages—some fifty in all . . . with a view to economy of space" (v). The *Encyclopaedia* article was written and published in 1882. There is a table of contents and an index of names.

The book reviews the history of Aristotelian logic, then moves to a discussion of Bacon and Descartes, through the empiricism of John Locke, David Hume, John Stuart Mill, and Étienne Condillac, then to Gottfried Wilhelm Leibniz and Immanuel Kant. After a criticism of the chief schools of logic, he provides a bibliography of the histories of logic, the Hindu systems of logic, and Ramus.

English Literature

NICHOL, JOHN. 1862–89. GUL MS Gen. 277. 43 lectures dated January 9, 1877, to April 4, 1877. No page numbers, but a good index with subjects. Handwriting legible, binding good. *English Literature. Prof. Nichol's Lectures, 1877. Taken by William Martin, Glasgow.*

Professor Nichol says at the outset that the course has three branches: "a course of philological lectures at a separate hour," and "a series of lectures on composition and style that will begin tomorrow." He then lists the books that are to be read in the course. In addition to collections of English authors, he suggests George Campbell and Richard Whately on rhetoric and Lord Kames' *Essay on Criticism*. Lectures 1–8 cover the general subject of style and the principles of criticism, with lecture 8 giving the eight rules for criticism and critical writing. The lectures that follow are an overview of English literature starting with Ossian, moving then to Ambrose, Bede, and Alcuin. He continues through Chaucer, with a long section on Shakespeare, concluding with Francis Beaumont and John Fletcher.

This is a rather undistinguished overview of English literature, but this set of notes is of interest because it is from the first course in English literature at the University of Glasgow, because of the list of textbooks, and because of the exams sprinkled throughout the lectures. (See the exam with lecture 9 and the exam at the end of the course.) The exam

125

questions merely ask that the material presented in the lectures and the readings be repeated: "1. Give an outline of the plot of one of Shakespeare's tragedies. 2. Name the leading Scotch and English authors of the 15th and 16th centuries with the titles and subjects of their works."

NICHOL, JOHN. 1862–89. GUL BG 57-c.17.4. Bound in with a number of other publications, many of them inaugural lectures. 32 pages. Printing clear, binding deteriorating. *Inaugural Lecture to the Course of English Language and Literature in the University of Glasgow* by John Nichol. November 17, 1862. Glasgow: James Maclehose, 61 St. Vincent Street. 1862.

This lecture, delivered by the first professor of the newly established chair of English literature, is an interesting demonstration of the sense of responsibility that John Nichol felt. It also demonstrates that he felt that "composition" as it is now commonly called is an important part of the course. After a review of the history of English literature, he describes the late development of modern criticism, by which he means criticism of the English language. In this respect, he cites Leonard Cox's *The Arte or Crafte of Rhetoryke* (1524) as the earliest specimen of a critical work in English; he then lists Thomas Wilson's *Arte of Rhetorique* (1553) and George Puttenham's *Arte of English Poesie* (1589) (14). These examples, more than anything he says, demonstrate the concept of criticism at this time. It is closely connected with rhetoric and with poetry.

He divides the course under three main headings: English composition, English philology, English literature (16). In connection with composition, he echoes the old refrain "not a day passes without affording some instance of deficiency in an art which is essential . . . to success" (16). In pointing out the necessity for composition for the Scots, he quotes William Wordsworth as saying, "no Scotchman could write English," and adds, "although this exaggeration might be refuted, it indicates the defect of a nation trained more to oratory than to authorship, whose mental force is apt to outrun its taste" (17). He includes in composition "an acquaintance with the rules of composition and the canons of good taste" (17). He emphasizes the connection in modern philosophy between language (rhetoric), psychology, and ethics. In his discussion of the importance of the study of English literature, he stresses a theme reflected in his lectures—that literature cannot be studied without studying history.

His closing remarks emphasize the study of literature as both patriotic and embracing a moral vision.

The study of our own literature encourages the best sort of patriotism, our pride in our great men. It enlarges our ideas by enabling us to penetrate into their minds, and stimulates us to emulate, by setting forth, the qualities which made them great. It takes away our jealousies, by holding up standards, in following which we have need to resign our self-complacency, and waive a little of our individual claims. It tones our rancour down, by showing us the common grounds on which we may meet and shake hands. The study of works which time has allowed to last, is, above all, the best corrective to the impatience of an age so productive of many which are in their very nature ephemeral, more noted for critical acuteness than magnanimity, more diffuse than intense in feeling, in thought more rapid than profound, more mindful of the shortness of life than the length of art. (32)

NICHOL, JOHN. 1862–89. *English Composition*. In the Literature Primers Series, ed. J. R. Green. London: Macmillan and Co., 1879. 28 pages. GUL ENG D 408 NIC.

It is interesting that John Nichol, the first professor of English literature at the University of Glasgow, published this small (three and one-half by four inches) primer of English composition, which he obviously felt was within the purview of his teaching responsibilities. The book is divided into five parts:

Part I: Introductory: sentences and punctuation.
Part II: Accuracy and Purity: diction and correct grammar.

Part III: Clearness and Precision: simplicity, brevity, tautology, and precision.
Part IV: Strength and Grace: figures of speech.
Part V: Versification: Rhyme, Alliteration, Tone, Accent, Metrical Feet and English Metres.

This book on composition deals entirely with matters of style and has completely lost its connection with the classical tradition of invention, arrangement, and of course, with memory and delivery. It is also marked by such terms as "the laws of style," "correct grammar," and "propriety." In speaking of "the laws of style," Nichol compares them to the rules of "civil discipline, of good conduct and good manners, laws that bind and laws that ought to bind us." Continuing the metaphor, he says that the rules of grammar are its imperative laws; "the canons of taste its manners" (15). He questions the accepted standard of usage as the sole standard of accuracy and taste (16).

NICHOL, JOHN and W. S. M'CORMICK. 1862–89. *Questions and Exercises on English Composition*. London: Macmillan and Co., 1890. 124 pages. GUL. ENG D 413 NIC.
This small book of questions and exercises was written to accompany Nichol's *English Composition* with headings that match that text. He asserts that the questions are "largely drawn from Papers set on the subject to the classes of English Literature in the University of Glasgow during the last twenty-seven years" (5). He asserts that they "are of various degrees of difficulty, beginning with comparatively simple points of Grammar, and afterwards dealing with some of the more controverted delicacies of Taste" (5).

NICHOL, JOHN. 1862–89. GUL 1-i.25/4. Bound in with a number of other publications on the subject of education in nineteenth-century Scotland. 40 pages. Printing clear, binding good. *The Teaching of English Literature in Our Universities and its Relation to Philology*. An Inaugural Address by John Nichol, Emeritus Professor of English Language and Literature in the University of Glasgow. Liverpool: F. E. Gibbons, 1891.

This address, delivered two years after his retirement from the chair at Glasgow, is an answer to remarks made to the Royal Commission ("as always imperiously," Nichol states [16]) by a Mr. Freeman, professor of theology at Aberdeen. The particular point that is of interest in this study is Nichol's answer to "Mr. Freeman's false postulate that *there is no standard of taste*" (21). Nichol remarks that this "presumption is fatal to the hope of genuine instruction in any art" (21). He then states that the "object of rational criticism" is "to contradict the hasty, to anticipate the sounder and slower verdicts of the world, to put men in a frame of mind to correct their own mistakes and those of their less well-enlightened contemporaries, to train them to fine feeling in art, as to good feeling in life" (22). So with style, he continues, "grammar prescribes that it must be accurate, logic enjoins that it should be clear, taste that it ought to be graceful. Mere usage is a shifting canon" (24).

Nichol concludes with one of his strongly held beliefs: "that the History and the Literature of every country are necessary comments on each other, and cannot be studied altogether apart" (32). One of his final paragraphs repeats his theme of nationalism and the moral view that the study of literature encourages (see also GUL BG 57-c.17).

6

The Universities of the North: St. Andrews and Aberdeen

The universities of the Scottish north, Aberdeen and St. Andrews, shared their medieval beginnings with Glasgow. Although adhering to the Scottish philosophy of education with their urban counterparts at Glasgow and Edinburgh, the universities of the north differed radically in their development. R. D. Anderson determined that, in 1864, 1866, and 1868, three-quarters of the students at Aberdeen came from the northeast; of these, 17.5 percent came from the city of Aberdeen, the rest from the surrounding counties. The remainder of the students came from the Highlands and overseas (*Student Community* 7). There were no school-leaving examinations, and the rural schools did not keep their students beyond the age of fifteen, meaning that these students often arrived at the universities at thirteen or fourteen, even younger than those at Edinburgh and Glasgow. They had early run out of teachers and subjects in their country parishes, and they came to the universities to further their education. They were generally poor, and, when the university common tables were abandoned, they were forced to exist on meager rations (Mountford 12). The student body also included a fair number of older students from the merchant and laboring classes within the city itself.

The bursary competition, open to all, was a famous institution and resulted in a form of scholarship for students who had been coached by their local rectors to sit for the examinations.

Largely a test in Latin composition, it was given in October. These examinations were described by one sixteen-year-old who, with four friends in 1818, was "deemed fit by good old Johnie Cruikshank, Rector of Banff Academy," to sit for the examinations (Leslie 8).

> Behold then, us five, seated in the large College Hall, along with ninety others, Latin Dictionary (Ainsworth's), pens, ink and paper—a professor presiding who was now and then relieved by another, for we were never left to our own devices. . . . We worked on steadily and had the prescribed work finished by evening. . . . A few days afterwards, all Competitors were ordered to attend at the College Hall, and we did so with beating hearts. The Professors all met—"A Terrible show"—and the competitors and a vast number of ladies and gentlemen were assembled. The scene altogether was impressive. The gravestone of Bishop Elphinstone, the founder of the College, had a conspicuous place in the centre of the Hall, and Principal Jack calling out the name of each successful competitor he had to proceed and stand uncovered on the "Bludstone." 20 yearly for four years was the highest bursary; the others were for lesser sums, varying from 18 to 5 and it might be about thirty in number. (9)

This student won a bursary, but "wee Johnie Robertson" did not, nor did "one competitor aged 42," who had "made use of the word 'realie' and that condemned in a great degree his version." According to Leslie, "he tried next year and got a high one," carefully avoiding any Scotticisms. He was a "ditcher and labourer from Rosshire and was a good Greek scholar and Latin too" (9).

The Scottish professorial world of the nineteenth century was like a small and intimate club, with membership often passed down from father to son. William Spalding went from St. Andrews to Glasgow, John Veitch moved to Glasgow, and the Ritchie and Beattie families taught for three generations. John Lee went from Aberdeen to St. Andrews and then to the principalship at Edinburgh; and Herbert J. C. Grierson, holder of the first chair of English literature at Aberdeen, moved from there to Edinburgh.

131

The northern universities were often the training grounds for young professors who then moved on to Edinburgh or Glasgow. Professors could hold their positions for life and were assigned assistants when they became too old, too sick, or just too occupied with other projects to fulfill their duties. The assistants were paid by the professors. The letters from John Lee (who was teaching both at St. Andrews and at King's College) to his assistant, Alexander Simpson, give an accurate account of this practice (AUL K. 206). Assistants often served years reading yellowed sets of notes of an aging professor in the hopes of eventually gaining lifetime tenure to the chair. Alexander Bain in his *Autobiography* described his duties as assistant to George Glennie. He was expected to read Glennie's lectures verbatim but found it difficult "to hold the attention of the class" (119). He began to insert his own material to relieve his own and the students' boredom, but he finally resigned in 1844.

> I had grave doubts about continuing another year; partly because I thought my time was not sufficiently rewarded, unless I could look to be his successor, and partly also because I dreaded having in the class a grandson of his own—whose notes he might ask to see, and thereby become more completely aware of my deviations from his lectures. (123)

Often professors were given very pleasant houses on the university grounds. A university professorship was a much sought-after position.

The Universities of St. Andrews and Dundee

St. Andrews, the oldest of the Scottish universities, was founded in 1410, modeled on the French by Bishop Henry Wardlaw of St. Andrews, who had studied at Paris and Orléans. Hitherto, Scottish students had attended Oxford or the Scot's college at Paris. St. Andrews afforded the first opportunity for Scottish students to attend their own university. In its early days, it consisted of three colleges, St. Salvator, St. Leonard, and St. Mary's. In the middle of the eighteenth century, when the student body had dwindled to only a few students, the two arts colleges were combined. At the same time, the regenting system was abandoned and the professorial system of specialists was slowly introduced. Even into the eighteenth century, however, the professors held their positions only briefly and moved with ease from one course to another and from one school to another. St. Andrews has remained small, almost going out of existence in the nineteenth century. In 1876, the college had only 130 students out of a total of five thousand at Scottish universities as a whole, and the Royal Commission strongly suggested that it "do more to bring itself into line with the needs of the age" (Shafe 10). Isolated in a small village, buffeted by winds from the North Sea, St. Andrews has nevertheless long boasted a loyal following. One nineteenth-century student recalled St. Andrews as having plenty of room—in contrast to the black old quads of Glasgow. He spoke affectionately of the "sea, the links, the fallen fanes, the gardens of St. Leonard's, the friendly little grey town, with the wide wind-swept street, the little set of gay idle boys who wore the scarlet gown" (Lang 29). Today, it is a small residential university drawing students from upper-class English and Scottish families.

The University of Dundee, just north of St. Andrews, shared its early history with that university. At the beginning of the nineteenth century, Dundee had a population of fewer than ten thousand, which increased by 1881 to 142,000. It had become a thriving commercial center, and the University College of Dundee was founded by a trust deed at that time. St. Andrews was still in the doldrums, isolated and conservative, and it seemed a natural and mutually beneficial arrangement for the two colleges to merge. In 1897, the University College at Dundee became affiliated with the University of St. Andrews. A medical school was established at Dundee in 1898 and the two continued to share professors, funds, and students. The partnership was not without some bitterness on both sides, however. One alumnus of St. Andrews expressed the view of many when he remarked that he did not wish his alma mater to be "tied up with strings of jute around its neck and drowned in pots of marmalade" (Shafe 8). The remark caught the glaring differences between the communities—Dundee a thriving commercial center and St. Andrews still isolated, still conservative, almost moribund.

It is difficult to trace the course of rhetoric at St. Andrews and Dundee. From 1862 to 1892, by fiat of the Royal Commission, instruction in rhetoric and English literature was given in the logic and metaphysics course. Although there is only one set of notes from that period, from Andrew Seth (often indexed under Pringle-Pattison), it can be safely assumed that William Spalding, who first taught at Edinburgh, lectured on rhetoric at St. Andrews using the principles in his *Treatise on Rhetoric,* which he wrote in Edinburgh and published in 1839 (GUL BC 28-d.13). The set of essays from his class at Edinburgh also provides insights into his teaching methods (EUL Ms. Gen. 769 D). In 1881, a chair of English language and literature was included in the original foundation of the University of Dundee, and Professors Thomas Gilray and William Symington McCormick taught that course at both Dundee and St. Andrews. It is this thread that I have followed in my index search for rhetoric. The following professors taught at St. Andrews during the eighteenth century in the logic and metaphysics course, which included rhetoric, and in the English language and literature course at Dundee.

St. Andrews
1778   William Barron
1804   James Hunter
1845   William Spalding
1860   John Veitch
1864   Thomas Spencer Baynes
1887   Andrew Seth (often called Pringle-Pattison)
1894   David Ritchie

Dundee
1882   Thomas Gilray
1890   William Symington McCormick

Many of the professors of logic and metaphysics at St. Andrews held their positions only briefly and moved on to other posts. James Hunter and Thomas Spencer Baynes held their posts for extended periods. William Barron's two-volume *Lectures on Belles Lettres and Logic* was published in London in 1806 and provides

134

a good outline of his course. We have our best understanding of James Hunter's course from his evidence before the Royal Commission in 1827, midway in his long tenure of forty-one years. He had one class that he divided equally between logic and rhetoric. He described his class in rhetoric: "I begin with considering Language, or the properties of Style; then Spoken Language, or Eloquence; and lastly Written Language, comprehending the most approved compositions in prose and verse" (*Evidence, Aberdeen* 121). He added that he had examinations for about twenty minutes each day, presumably oral, which he found to be "the only way of bringing home completely" the substance of the lectures. He also assigned subjects for essays and gave prizes "out of his own pocket" (121–22). He attested that there were "a great many essays" written in his class. One of the commissioners suggested that his course might be improved by following George Jardine's method of an additional hour for examination, but Hunter refused to commit himself on that point. In answer to the question of what books he was in the habit of recommending, he replied, "Reid's *Inquiry* and his other essays on the intellectual powers, Stewart's *Philosophy* and Alison on Taste" (123). Appended to his testimony is a lengthy description of his logic and rhetoric course, which he subsequently submitted to the commission. He suggested the close connection between the two subjects at the point "where the analysis and investigation of our intellectual faculties seem to shade gradually off into the theory of expressing the results of their operation, and where the regulation of our reasoning powers is connected, by an invisible transition with the rules of correct composition" (124). Hunter's rhetoric course seems to have been largely concerned with grammar, which he called the principles of criticism, and style, which embraced perspicuity and ornament, which, in turn, included a long description of figures. He concluded with "a short account of Written Language, comprehending the most elegant and approved compositions in prose and verse—namely, History, Letterwriting, Fiction, and Dialogue, in the one; and in the other, Pastoral, Lyric, Elegiac, Didactic, Descriptive, Epic, and Dramatic Poetry" (125). This course like many of the others of the period contains a section called "Eloquence," which he fails to describe but may be presumed to be a short outline of classical rhetoric in connection with oratory. This part of these rhetoric courses becomes smaller and smaller as the century progresses.

William Spalding, who followed Hunter, came from Edinburgh. During most of his time at St. Andrews, he was in "delicate physical health, though with an active and fertile brain." Our best record of his course is from the notes taken by a student at the University of Edinburgh.

Spalding is followed by John Veitch, who after only four years moved on to Glasgow, where we can find a record of his course in the excellent set of notes in GUL MS. Gen. 40/1–2.

Thomas Spencer Baynes then held the chair for twenty-three years and was fondly remembered by his students. His course is called "English Literature" in the manuscript memoirs of one his students, who testified that Baynes gave them essays to write, with a choice of subjects, which the students then read aloud in class. This same student missed a class and requested to see Baynes' lecture notes, which he described as containing only "hints and catch phrases for suggestion in extemporary speaking" ("Autobiographical Notes by A. Allan," Archives at the University of St. Andrews).

There followed a succession of professors who held the chair for only three years each. Andrew Seth served as assistant to Alexander Campbell Fraser at the University of Edinburgh and returned after his brief tenure at St. Andrews to the chair of logic at that university, a position he held for twenty-eight years. He is described in the *Dictionary of National Biography* as "a successful although scarcely a great teacher. A shy man, unready of speech, he hugged the shelter of his manuscript, reading it beautifully to large classes which sometimes were almost openly restive." David Ritchie was the last professor to hold the chair. All of these men published widely—Ritchie in political science, Baynes on Shakespeare, and Andrew Seth on Robert Browning.

With the establishment of the chair of English language and literature at Dundee, English composition and rhetoric became the responsibility of Professors Gilray and McCormick, the first holders of the chair St. Andrews. During this period, however, Dundee had no power to award degrees, and students were prepared for the degree examinations at London University. Thus,

Dundee, at this time, was termed a "teaching college," operating like other institutions in England that provided instruction but did not award degrees. London University, on the other hand, was in its early years a degree-granting institution that provided examinations but no instruction. It was not until 1897 that University College Dundee became a part of the University of St. Andrews, thus allowing students to obtain a degree.

Thomas Gilray studied under David Masson at Edinburgh and served for three years as his assistant. In 1882, Gilray took up the post of professor of English literature and language at the University of Dundee. He is listed in the 1884 calendar as teaching English literature on Mondays and Wednesdays from 3:30 to 4:30; history of the English language on Tuesdays for one hour; modern history and the constitutional history of England from 3:30 to 4:30 on Thursdays; and English composition and rhetoric for one hour on Friday afternoons. In this description, he asserts that the work of the rhetoric class will consist of practice in English composition, which "will be written in the Class-room, [and] which will be taken home for examination by the Professor, carefully corrected, valued, and returned" (55). In addition to assigning longer papers for the students to write at home, "the professor will read extracts from the greatest masters of English Prose and will aim at cultivating a sense of style and purity of taste" (55). This will be followed by "a systematic study of the rules of correct writing, and the principles of rhetoric and literature" (55). The text for the course is Bain's *English Composition and Rhetoric, A Manual*. Gilray held the post at Dundee for seven years before leaving to take up a position at Otago University in New Zealand.

Gilray's successor in the chair was William Symington McCormick, who lectured at both Dundee and St. Andrews. His classes were small, seldom more than fifteen students, as most of the university classes were at that time. The 1890–91 calendar lists the four classes taught by McCormick as English literature, English composition and rhetoric, history of the English language, and Anglo-Saxon. The composition and rhetoric description is brief.

This class is intended to give instruction in the elements of Style, and in the practice of English Composition. The

Lectures will deal with the more common violations of grammar, purity and propriety of vocabulary, strength and grace of style, and the general principles of Rhetoric. A Text-Book will be studied in connection with the Lectures, and Exercises and Essays will be prescribed from time to time.

The suggested textbook is Nichol's *English Composition*. In the 1893 calendar, a lecturer has been assigned to Professor McCormick to teach the class in English literature, which he is now teaching at both Dundee and St. Andrews. In an address to the college at Dundee, he spoke eloquently of the study of literature and of the need for training the aesthetic sense for the "eye that has been trained to skim the news of the morning paper" only. He sounds very modern, however, in his advice to students.

Guidance will doubtless be of service, but we must never deceive ourselves in regarding the opinions or criticisms of others as our own or even as copies. For each of us, according to the limitations and individuality of his character, will make from the original creation of the poet a creation of his own. (UD Recs. A/119 UD)

He admitted in his report to the principal that "the evening course of lectures was poorly attended" and that he proposed "to offer a class next year on the 'Principles of English Composition'" (81). In the calendar for the next year, he reported to the principal that the class was attended by twenty-two students and "that a great deal of work was done by about half the class" (87). He adds another lecturer, "R.K.," in 1895, and there is no further record in the calendars of the course in English composition after this date. McCormick applied for but did not get the chair of English literature at St. Andrews; he was, however, later asked to be secretary of the newly established Carnegie Trust for the Universities of Scotland. He continued in that post for a number of years and was influential in university reforms until he died in 1930.

The University of Aberdeen

The nineteenth-century University of Aberdeen also had medieval roots. King's College was founded in 1495 by the Bishop of Aberdeen under a papal bull. After the Reformation, there was a movement away from the Catholic college, and in 1593, William Keith sought an act of Parliament to found Marischal College. For nearly three hundred years, the colleges operated side by side. They were united as the University of Aberdeen in 1860, with arts and divinity at King's and law and medicine at Marischal. The fusion was nominal for many years.

The eighteenth-century student community at Aberdeen, as described by R. D. Anderson, was different from those of the Universities of Glasgow and Edinburgh and markedly different from that of the English institutions. Only 35 percent of the students had fathers in the professions; 14.5 percent had fathers in commerce and industry. A full 50 percent came from homes of agricultural and working-class families (*Student Community* 138). In the seventeenth century, students were fined for speaking in the vernacular (AUL MS M 391), and proper English and good manners—"knife-and-fork" education—were sometimes considered part of the professors' responsibility. Principal William R. Pirie inaugurated an annual breakfast where the presence of professors' wives was considered a civilizing influence. Most professors, however, "took the view that the private lives and extra-curricular activities of students were not their business" (33).

The tradition of wearing the red gown and the trencher did not last long in the windy northern climate of Aberdeen, but when it was worn, to be correct, the gown was supposed to be old and ragged. "Gown tearing" and crushing on the stairs were part of the ritual suffered by first-year students. Students normally attended lectures for four hours every day and then went to their lodgings to work or read. As R. D. Anderson describes, the lectures were governed by well-established social traditions.

> It was customary for professors to start each lecture with a short prayer, to give occasional disciplinary reprimands or moral advice, and to bring out venerable jokes for student approval. Student feelings were made clear by foot-stamping or "ruffing" for approval and foot-scraping for disapproval. There was also a tradition of lively behavior before the professor arrived, which took the everyday form of communal singing, and the more boisterous one

of "passing up" students over the heads of their fellows from the front of the tiered lecture theatre to the back. (16)

The lecture hours were broken by visits to the baker's shop for the traditional "jam scones," and popular professors were showered with gifts while unpopular ones received rough treatment. R. D. Anderson cites the case of a Latin professor who was "followed to his home by a jeering procession and pelted with stones" (16). When Alexander Bain was elected to the rectorship in 1881 in a highly controversial election, his introductory lecture was interrupted by "continual noise from bagpipes, trumpets, hooters and other improvised instruments, and fireworks were thrown as well as dried peas." After half an hour, he abandoned his speech (28). In spite of the customary rowdiness of the students, the University of Aberdeen was intellectually alive during the eighteenth and nineteenth centuries. There were heated debates on subjects of the day, and a number of extracurricular societies and newspapers thrived during this period.

Before the visitations of the Royal Commissioners in 1827, degrees at both King's and Marischal had been conferred loosely and carried little value. There was no record at King's College of any student not passing the degree examination, an examination that was neither long nor difficult. At Marischal College, the same set of questions was "answered for all years," and the professor of moral philosophy dictated copies of "both questions and answers to the candidates," which they then heard the students "recite by rote" (P. J. Anderson, *Studies* 15). A student often attended the university for only two years and then entered his father's business or returned to the farm. Not uncommonly, he might return in later years to sit in on lectures or even to take a degree.

The professors at King's and Marischal formed a small and intimate club, most of them having been a part of the regenting system that was retained at King's until the beginning of the nineteenth century largely because of Thomas Reid's influence. The masters had agreed to continue the regenting system, which, as stated earlier, had been by this time abandoned at the other Scottish universities. It was justified as "more beneficial to the Students," though "more laborious for the Professors," because every Professor of Philosophy in this University is also tutor to those who study under him; has the whole direction of their studies, the training of their minds, and the oversight of their manners. . . . It may reasonably be supposed that a Professor, in three years, may acquire an acquaintance with the temper and genius of his pupils, and an authority over them, which may be of great use to them, and yet is not to be expected in the course of one Session. (Qtd. in P. J. Anderson, *Studies* 13)

It was further agreed that the regent was better able to judge the progess the student had made over the vacation and, although it was admitted that a professor who taught only one branch of philosophy would have "more leisure to make improvement in it for the benefit of the learned world," still a professor ought to be "sufficiently qualified to teach all that his pupils can learn in Philosophy in the course of three Sessions" (qtd. in P. J. Anderson, *Studies* 13). In 1800, the professorships of mathematics, natural philosophy, and moral philosophy were assigned to three regents. Remnants of the system still persisted, however, well into the nineteenth century, as regents who had served as generalists became professors in specialized subjects. What was taught by the professors, however, was influenced more by the professor himself than by the title of the course. Rhetoric was generally taught in the chair of moral philosophy and logic, and, when the commissioners directed English to be taught by the logic professor, it could be either composition or literature or it could be both. In the case of Alexander Bain, it became basic composition and psychology. After the union of King's and Marischal as the University of Aberdeen in 1860, English literature and composition were taught by the professors of logic, Alexander Bain and William Minto, until the establishment of the Chalmers Professorship of English Literature in 1893. The professors, the dates they arose, and the subjects are as follows:

KING'S, MORAL PHILOSOPHY AND LOGIC
1800   Robert Eden Scott
1811   William Jack
1817   Daniel Dewar

141

1819   Andrew Alexander
1820   John Lee
1821   Hercules Scott

MARISCHAL, MORAL PHILOSOPHY AND LOGIC
1796   George Glennie
1841   Alexander Bain
1844   William R. Pirie
1845   William Martin

ABERDEEN, LOGIC
1860   Alexander Bain
1880   William Minto

ABERDEEN, ENGLISH LITERATURE
1894   Herbert John Clifford Grierson

We have two sets of notes from Robert Eden Scott, who was appointed a regent at King's in 1788, served as coprofessor of natural philosophy, Greek, and mathematics before his appointment to the chair of moral philosophy in 1800. One set appears to be his own notes; the other is a set of notes taken by a student. We also have his small printed volume *Elements of Rhetoric*, published in 1802, a much more readable copy of his course notes.

Another source of information about his course comes from the evidence presented to the Royal Commission in 1827. In his testimony, he complains that during one year he is expected to instruct his students in logic, in moral and political philosophy, and in rhetoric and belles lettres. He suggests that there be a separate chair in logic and rhetoric, adding that he delivers a short course of lectures on rhetoric starting at the beginning of December. This treatment of rhetoric seems to be completely divorced from his emphasis on composition, which pervades the course.

He provides a detailed description of his course. The students attend from 8:30 to 9:00 and are examined viva voce on the lecture of the previous day and also read the answers that they have written on the questions presented during the lecture. Between 11:00 and 12:00, the lecture is presented; between 3:00 and 4:00 questions are prescribed and "a considerable part of this hour is likewise occupied in the practice of composition" (*Evidence, Aberdeen* 40). He explains:

> For this purpose, certain subjects of essay [sic] are pre-
> scribed by the Professor publicly in the class, and a time
> fixed, before which the essays must be left by the authors
> at the Professor's house. After being examined in private
> by the Professor, and the inaccuracies, whether of
> thought or composition, carefully marked, they are re-
> turned to the authors, by whom they are read publicly in
> the class; their inaccuracies are pointed out, and com-
> mented on, and an opinion as to their merits or defects
> publicly expressed. (40)

Professor Scott comments that his system of requiring written answers to the questions is original with him. He adds that the paper subjects are generally connected with the lectures and that the early papers are read by the professor without mentioning the name of the author, "to save, as far as possible, the feelings of individuals." He echoes the familiar complaint about errors in grammar and spelling and "even in orthography."

We have very little information about William Jack, Daniel Dewar, or Andrew Alexander except for the small book by Dewar which appears to have been taken from his course on moral philosophy. It contains no information on rhetoric. At the union of King's and Marischal, Dewar was turned down in favor of George Glennie, who apparently took over the chair of moral philosophy and logic at that time.

John Lee was appointed professor of moral philosophy at King's in 1820, after having served as professor of church history at St. Andrews for eight years. His two sets of notes are interesting because he appears to have mailed his lectures from St. Andrews to Alexander Simpson, who then read them to the students at King's. They still bear the original postmarks, and the lectures are accompanied by a number of sometimes poignant personal letters. In 1837, he was appointed principal of St. Andrews, as his letters indicate, a position he resigned after only a few months. The second set of notes, of more interest to the rhetoric scholar, was delivered at Aberdeen and might well be the same set he used in the divinity class at Edinburgh, which he taught after he was appointed principal there in 1840. Lee is described by Sir Alexander Grant in his history of the University of Edinburgh as having "given to the world so little of what he knew" (273). Grant calls him a bibliomaniac, who "only accumulated the knowledge, without putting it into form" (274).

The curious sets of student notes from Hercules Scott's class are an interesting example of the kind of catechetical system employed in the Scottish universities and may well be an example of the kinds of questions and answers that Hercules Scott used. The professor read a series of prepared questions (often repeated year after year or read verbatim by his assistant). This student apparently took down the questions and answers with great conscientiousness. This is the only set of such questions and answers that I have encountered in my search through these student notes. The subject of rhetoric has disappeared from these notes by this time, and the thread of rhetoric moves after the union of King's and Marischal to the courses of George Glennie and then to Alexander Bain.

George Glennie's testimony before the Royal Commission of 1827 is a study in contrast to Robert Eden Scott's described above. At Marischal College, Glennie served as the assistant to James Beattie and in 1803 took charge of the course on the occasion of Beattie's death. He in turn was served by deputies from 1840 to 1845, including Alexander Bain and William R. Pirie.

In his testimony before the commission just three days after Scott's, Glennie too complains of the subjects he is required to teach, asserting that they "might furnish employment for three or four different Professors" (*Evidence, Aberdeen* 106). He describes the course in considerable detail, including the last department, which includes rhetoric.

> To rhetoric is referred the theory of language, introduced in an early part of the course; the difference between ancient and modern criticism, as far as the latter is denominated philosophical; the nature of poetical composition, as distinguished from prose; the nature and use of tropes

and figures, and the rules for the structure of the various sorts of periods and sentences. (105)

He also assigns themes and exercises, which he does not seem to associate with rhetoric anymore than with any of the other subjects in the course. He does not have his students criticize each others' work but adds that the examinations are of assistance to the lecturer "because he can know by the examination when he is understood, and when he is not understood" (105).

He defends his practice of dictating notes, saying that the subjects that he is discussing are so abstract that the students could not answer his questions if he did not dictate. He says that he has attempted to teach without dictating notes, but that much more time must then be spent in examining the students. Having just interviewed Robert Eden Scott three days before, the commissioners asked if he had thought of publishing a synopsis of his notes. As far as I could discover, he never did so.

Certainly, Alexander Bain, although well known to students of the history of rhetoric, comes down in the literature as a split personality. He is remembered in Scotland with reverence for his course in psychology, but he was heartily disliked by his students of composition. Unfortunately, his bequest to American rhetoric is through his principles of composition. Although we have no student notes from Bain, his ideas are well documented in his extensive writings, primarily in his *Autobiography* and *Practical Essays*. He covered his teaching ideas in *English Composition and Rhetoric* and in *A Higher English Grammar* with its *Companion to Higher English Grammar*. He held the chair of moral philosophy and logic from 1841 to 1843 at Marischal and was the first holder of the newly established chair of logic after the union of the University of Aberdeen in 1860.

In a special issue of *Alma Mater,* the University of Aberdeen's magazine, in memory of Alexander Bain, Professor W. M. Ramsay, in an understatement, remembered Bain's English class as "extremely uninteresting."

The class remains in my memory as a sort of nightmare; I sat through it, except for twelve absences, dumb and stupid, unable even to take notes, so unintelligible and wea-

145

risome was everything; and the most extraordinary fact about it was that I was placed 21 in the class list. I ought to have been 96 in the list: there were 97 in the class, but one was, I believe, worse than me. As it was, I was sorry for No. 22. (8)

He continued in the very next paragraph to describe Bain's logic class:

> Very different was the Logic Class. From the first sentence that the Professor uttered, one felt that one was in the presence of a master, a man of power. It was a revelation and an inspiration to me; and I have ever since dated the first real step in my education from that class. . . . in the first of those five years, I was absolutely happy for five hours every week, viz., the five hours of lecturing in the Logic Class. (8)

Bain maintained that the field of English literature could not be covered in sixty half-hour lectures, and as a result his "English course confined itself to an exhaustive handling of rhetoric" and the literature "was not even touched upon" (*Alma Mater* 5). His former students did not remember his English course with any affection: "Nothing more dismal than his excursions into literary criticism has probably ever been done: and his book on Rhetoric remains a monument of totally misdirected effort" (*Alma Mater* 10). This former student, who did not sign his name, finally attributed the "atrophied condition of the Aberdonian in the domain of letters" to Bain's malevolent influence. These quotes, gleaned from the issue of the magazine *Alma Mater* in memory of Alexander Bain, among a series of eulogies, are eloquent testimony about Bain's English course.

Alexander Bain is best and certainly most kindly remembered for his contributions to psychology. J. C. Flugel described Bain as "the author of the first textbook on psychology written in the modern manner" (80). L. S. Hearnshaw placed Bain halfway between the mental philosophy of the eighteenth and early nineteenth centuries and the scientific psychology of the twentieth (3). Under the heading "Logic," the 1866–67 calendar listed

Bain as having two classes: one in logic and the other in English, which met one hour a day on alternate days. "The subjects are—the higher Elements of English Grammar; the Principles of Rhetoric, applied to English Composition; and some portion of the History of English Literature, from the reign of Elizabeth" (19). Alexander Bain was highly influential in American rhetoric, and his composition textbooks, especially *English Composition and Rhetoric,* have been held responsible for the emphasis on the topic sentence and the organic paragraph that turned writing into a rule-based formula that, according to several modern theorists, forced a stranglehold on students' writing in the first part of the twentieth century. American scholars, such as Robert J. Connors, Donald C. Stewart, and Richard Braddock, have disparaged the work of Bain, so that he has become what Andrea Lunsford calls "a popular whipping boy." Jon Harned holds Bain "responsible for the impoverishment of rhetoric in the late nineteenth century" (42).

Bain, in his *English Composition and Rhetoric,* defined the paragraph as a "division of discourse next above the sentence" and as a collection of sentences with "unity of purpose" (91). He explained that "unity in a paragraph implies a sustained purpose, and forbids digressions and irrelevant matter" (112). Comparing the paragraph to the sentence, he advised that "principal and subordinate statements should have their relative importance clearly indicated" (121). From these principles the twentieth-century compositionists derived the concept of the paragraph marked by unity, coherence, and emphasis. The idea of the topic sentence comes from Bain's description of the opening sentence, which is "expected to indicate the scope of the paragraph" (108). Each of these principles is accompanied by copious examples and allowance for many exceptions, particularly in the placement and occurrence of the topic sentence. The exceptions have been largely overlooked by modern composition theorists. Alfred Kitzhaber wrote, "Bain was, however, characteristically a dogmatic writer. He nearly always preferred to express himself categorically, seldom allowing any latitude for other interpretations" (247). A close reading of Bain does not confirm this opinion, although his principles as adopted by later compositionists may indeed have become dogmatic. Bain was teaching a group of students who needed to be taught English. His influence is most strongly felt in the teaching of basic writers in modern composition. As a highly influential figure in the field of composition and rhetoric, he deserves more careful and more sympathetic study.

Upon Bain's death in 1880, William Minto assumed the chair of logic. He had been a student of Bain, and for some years he was editor of the *Examiner* and a contributor to many of the London journals. He brought to Aberdeen his acquaintance with London literary life. He taught the course much as Bain had taught it, using Bain's books on composition and literature, but the course took on life as he brought to it his own love of literature. The 1888 calendar describes the English class as meeting one hour three times a week. "Lectures are delivered on the objects and methods of Grammar and Philology; the elements and principles of Style; and the methods of the historical study of Literature. A period of English Literature is discussed in detail" (53).

Like Bain, Minto's forte was logic. "English he knew well must ever be a secondary and non-essential part of the curriculum, the refuge of the passmen or the hold of a few" (P. J. Anderson, *Aurora* 59). However, the English composition course combined with logic survived until the establishment of the Chalmers Professorship of English Literature at Minto's death in 1893.

Herbert J. C. Grierson assumed the chair of English literature in 1894. Minto had hoped to succeed to that chair, but the appointment was awarded to Grierson, who spent a year studying English literature before he took over the chair one year after it was established. In 1899, the calendar described Grierson's course as still containing the remnants of rhetoric in one part called "The Principles of Style and Principles of Criticism." The best record of this section of the course is contained in Marie W. Stuart's notes in EUL MS. Gen. 2096–97D taken when he taught at the University of Edinburgh. He was still using Bain's book *English Composition and Rhetoric*. His lectures, moving from words, to sentences, to paragraphs, and finally to expository compositions, were heavily influenced by Bain.

There is no further rhetoric taught in the logic course. The incongruity of combining the two subjects of logic and English became increasingly apparent under Minto. The Royal Commission had decreed that English should be taught at all four Scottish universities, and at Aberdeen it had been joined to the chair of

148

logic, since rhetoric, the subject most closely connected with English at the other universities, was taught in conjunction with logic. Nowhere did it appear more incongruous than at Aberdeen, where the rationale of the connection between rhetoric and logic had disappeared. P. J. Anderson, in *Aurora Borealis Academica*, published in 1899, stressed this fact:

> The commission that conjoined the subjects of English and logic in a single chair either had a cheerful belief in the ability of man, or was more likely perplexed by the lack of endowments. There is no natural affinity between the two subjects, and it cannot be said that Professor Bain was in any way seen at his best in the English class, though it was the careful work of a strong man. (58)

Bain, never a lover of fine literature, put his indelible mark on the English course, seeing it as his duty to his students to help them attain the niceties of proper English, especially important for the students from the northern regions. Having himself come from a strongly rural background, and having himself had to fight to overcome his Scotticisms, he felt it his duty to instruct his students in the same path to what he considered success. And Alexander Bain was not the man to shirk his responsibilities. His influence was widespread especially in the United States, where his composition theories were eagerly adopted as being ideally suited to the American student.

The Universities of the North: Archival Materials

Although regenting was abolished in 1753 at Marischal and in 1798 at King's, the system was still more or less in effect until the fusion of the two schools into the University of Aberdeen in 1860. Accordingly, a professor would move readily from one class to another, usually teaching a course for no more than two or three years and then possibly teaching it again some years later.

Consequently, it is difficult to find any orderly sequence in the professors or the courses. The records at the University of Aberdeen manuscript library are not clear. The system of professorships was not in effect until Alexander Bain took over the logic course in 1860. Rhetoric was included in the moral philosophy and logic course at both King's and Marischal and in the logic course at the University of Aberdeen. The notes from King's College are listed first, in the order of the professors on pages 141–42, although the regenting system makes this list less than completely accurate. The notes from Marischal again are listed according to the order of the professors on page 142. The courses from the University of Aberdeen appear in a more orderly fashion. The professor's name and the years of his professorship are followed by the library in which the manuscript is located, its call number, and any pertinent information about its condition, such as legibility, number of pages, or volumes. Libraries are abbreviated as follows: EUL, University of Edinburgh Library; GUL, University of Glasgow Library; AUL, University of Aberdeen Library; and NLS, National Library of Scotland. The exact inscription on the title page then follows in italics.

King's College, Aberdeen: Moral Philosophy and Logic

SCOTT, ROBERT EDEN. 1800–1811. AUL K. 190–91. 2 volumes: vol. 1, 216 pp.; vol. 2, 232 pp. Writing clear but very small, reading tedious. Paginated. No table of contents or index. Bindings good. *Vol. 1: Elements of Moral Philosophy for the Magistrand Class–1798.* His own notes.

"In treating of the general divisions of science, philosophy is considered of two kinds: the properties of the visible or corporeal world or incorporeal substance or mind as directly opposite to the body." The first branch is generally called natural philosophy; the second, moral philosophy, which also might be distinguished by the names "Somatology or Pneumatology—the first being terms used in the English language." Since the mind is a nobler work and of a higher order than the body, then "we see of what a dignified nature that science is which has the mind for its subject" (2). "Since the revival of literature" philosophers have almost all "given into the errors of the ancients . . . even when the true methods of philosophizing had been successfully pointed out by Bacon and pursued by Newton and his followers in the department of physics—the metaphysical branch" (3). Where Berkeley, Hume, and Locke cannot be freed from this imputation, it is to "our countryman, Reid, that we are to consider this science as indebted for a firm foundation and for having clearly pointed out the true mode in which alone it can be cultivated and established in a rank equally respectable with that of the other sciences"—that is, by observation and principally through the faculties of the mind (3). Scott speaks again of "the false mode of reasoning which philosophers have hiterto adopted" (5).

Part 1 of volume 1 is entitled "Theory of Mind or Pneumatology," and chapter 1 is subtitled "Psychology." It is divided into twelve sections: on perception and sensation (11); on memory (33); on conception (known by logicians as "simple apprehension") (42); on judgment (defined as an art of the mind whereby one thing is affirmed or denied by another) (53); on reasoning (a belief produced by induction or a connected series of dependent propositions) (57); on imagination and the association of ideas (follows Stuart's view of the imagination as "that power of the mind whereby we make a selection of the qualities and circumstances from a variety of different objects, external as well as intellectual" and combine these to form a new creation) (61); on moral perception (71); on action of consciousness (75); on action of volition and free agency (78); on action of selfish active principles (85); on action of social active principles (90); on natural theology and jurisprudence (98–121).

Part 2 of volume 1 is entitled "Practical Intellectual Science" and includes sections on ethics (122), jurisprudence (140), logic (165), and politics (175). This last chapter on politics includes such variable sections as "The Diversities of Men and the Effects of Climate," "The Origin of Society and Language," "Of the Progress of Arts and Commerce," "Of

Population and Finance (more properly called Political Science)," and "Of Government." On the back of each page are appropriate quotations.

Vol. 2: Notes upon Moral Philosophy for the Magistrand Class, 1798.

This volume appears to be exactly what it is called. It is a series of notes, carefully keyed to the sections of the lectures in volume 1 by roman numerals enlarging and detailing that material.

These two volumes would be well worth further study. This is a typical course in moral philosophy of the period, markedly reflecting the ideas of Thomas Reid and the Scottish school of common sense.

SCOTT, ROBERT EDEN. 1800–1811. AUL K. 192. 220 pages. Writing small but clear, binding good. *Elements of Rhetoric and Belles Lettres for the Magistrand Class, 1801.* His own notes.

Like so many professors of the period, Scott starts with a definition of rhetoric.

> By the term Rhetoric we propose to denominate the science which professes to explain those principles of our constitution to which the various kinds of literary composition are addressed, the manner of their operation as they influence the different faculties of the mind; and also the foundation of those practical rules which have yet been devised for the improvement of all the species of eloquence and literature. The same science is also sometimes denominated Criticism, Eloquence, or the Belles Lettres. (1)

Scott then notes that we should be able to derive rules to explain the success or want of success of any composition (2).

He continues with the complaint that is echoed and reechoed throughout these lectures: that there is "little information in the writings of the ancients" (2). He says that he must go to the names of Henry Home (Lord Kames), George Campbell, Alexander Gerard, Hugh Blair, and James

Beattie, to which must be added Edmund Burke and another whose name is unclear, as investigators of our "notions of the beautiful and sublime and of the faculty of Taste" (2).

Scott then considers "in treating the Science of Rhetoric . . . the various species of composition in reference to the different end which they have in view . . . to instruct, to please or to persuade" (3). He acknowledges Campbell's influence but collapses under one heading Campbell's second and third divisions: to enlighten the understanding, to please the imagination, to move the passions, and to influence the will. He moves on to a section on instruction in writing, divided into different types of composition: history, philosophy, language. The last section, entitled "Of Language," discusses purity, propriety, perspicuity, harmony, elegance, animation, and figures of speech.

Part 3 treats composition, whose object is to please, and begins with a section on taste (100–111). Section 2 treats the pleasures derived from composition (112). Then follow three sections on terror, pity, melancholy, joy, and other emotions (116–33). The remaining sections cover a large amount of territory and treat the ludicrous (133); the sublime (142); the beautiful (148); novelty (158); the nature and origin of poetry (163); the elegy, epigram, descriptive and didactic poetry (168); epic poetry (176); dramatic and pastoral poetry (182); and fable and romance (193).

This manuscript is very difficult to annotate because Scott constantly confuses the parts, sections, and numbering.

Part 4, "Of Composition Whose Object is to Persuade" (199), Scott avows, is "undoubtedly the noblest and frequently the most arduous to accomplish of them all" (199). Scott then brings in some Aristotle when he says that the speaker will be successful (and this is obviously oral) when "the hearer is not unfavorably disposed with regard to the speaker" and when he trusts the understanding, knowledge, or integrity of the speaker (200). These attributes are developed at considerable length in this introductory section. Scott concludes this set of lectures on rhetoric by considering two kinds of eloquence: that of the senate and bar (205) and lastly the eloquence of the pulpit (213).

153

SCOTT, ROBERT EDEN. 1800–1811. *Elements of Rhetoric, for the Use of the Students of King's College, Aberdeen.* Aberdeen: Printed by J. Chalmers and Co. 1802.

This small, thin volume is almost, word for word, identical to Scott's own lecture notes on rhetoric (AUL K. 190–191) but in much more easily read form. The University of Aberdeen Library has several copies of this text.

After an introduction on the nature of rhetoric, the ancient art, which "consisted rather in practical rules, than in scientific investigation," and the modern art to which "we owe a philosophical investigation of the science of Rhetoric, and an analysis of those faculties of the mind" (3), part 1 is entitled "Of Language" and is divided into three sections.

1. "Of the Qualities Essential to Good Style," under which is included purity, which is governed by "the practice of authors of established reputation, and whose works are neither of a very old, nor of a perfectly recent date"; propriety, and perspicuity (6).
2. "Of the Ornamental Qualities of Style," which includes the qualities of harmony (melody, rhythm, elegance, and animation) (11).
3. "Of Figurative Language," which includes the ordinary listing of figures of speech (19).

Part 2 is entitled "Of Compositions, Whose Object is to Instruct" and contains two sections: "Of the Mode of Conveying Instruction" and "Of History and Philosophical Composition." Part 3 is entitled "Of Composition, Whose Object is to Please" and is divided into four sections: "Of Taste" (31), "Of the Sources of Pleasure in Composition" (39), "Of the Sublime and Beautiful," concluding with a section on "Novelty" (40), "Of the Species of Composition Intended to Please." The third section has an Aristotelian flavor in its discussion of terror, pity, and melancholy. The fourth section deals almost exclusively with poetry.

Part 4, "Of Compositions, Whose Object is to Persuade," treats what Scott terms "the noblest, and frequently the most arduous to accomplish" (55). This treatment is

154

about oral language. Such terms as *speaker, hearer,* and *orator* are used throughout. Section 1 is entitled "Of the Proper Methods of Persuasion" (55) and the second and last section is entitled "Various Species of Public Speaking" (58). After a very brief treatment of the eloquence of the bar and the assembly, pulpit oratory is treated.

This text is not prescriptive and lacks the moralistic tone of other texts of the period.

DEWAR, DANIEL. 1817–19. *Elements of Moral Philosophy, and of Christian Ethics.* 2 volumes: vol. 1, 502 pp.; vol. 2, 598 pp. London: J. Duncan, Paternoster-Row, 1826.

This course on moral philosophy was written, the author asserts in the preface, for the students of moral philosophy, and more especially as preparatory to their entering on the study of sacred theology as well as "for Christians generally" (vi).

The two volumes concern the "ethical department of Moral Philosophy . . . with the first book wholly occupied with the character, perfections, and Providence of God" (i). Dewar states in the preface that "the usual method is, to treat first of the active powers of man, and afterwards to discourse concerning the being and attributes of God." In this course, he is reversing this order.

There is no logic or rhetoric contained in this two-volume set confined as the author says to the "ethical department of Moral Philosophy" (i).

LEE, JOHN. 1820–21. AUL K. 206. Moral Philosophy. Writing small and very difficult to read. Notes contained in a box. Each lecture bound separately. First lectures numbered 4–33, but only the early ones have page numbers. His own notes.

There is no title, but a note at the beginning of the lectures reads, "Lectures by Dr. John Lee, professor Moral Philosophy in King's College, 1820. Being at the same time professor of Church History in St. Andrews, he did not deliver these lectures in person, but they were posted to the Rev. Alexander Simpson who read them to the students." This introductory note is an interesting comment on the practices of the day. These lectures are by the same man who was himself a student who left notes behind at Edinburgh. He later became the principal at Edinburgh. The note also reinforces the idea that many of the professors read their lectures slowly and with pauses so that the students could take them down verbatim. These lectures, bearing the postmark of St. Andrews and the address to the Rev. Alexander Simpson at King's College, Aberdeen, are preceded by a letter from Lee to Simpson instructing him about how to cut the pages, apologizing for the "thinness" of the first lecture, and warning him that "I suspect that I must continue to send all my lectures in this way" since "my troubles here are not likely to end. Tho the postage will be great, they will reach you with continuity." He then asks him "to pick out questions from the 3 students in your hands."

Sometimes Lee's correspondence is more interesting than his lectures. At one point he writes: "I meant to say that prizes will be given to the two best essays on Patriotism—You may let it be understood that they will be presented by the Rector of the University of St. Andrews—I was this day unanimously selected to that office." In a later undated letter he writes:

> I am obliged to ask you to fill up the remainder of this lecture from Stewart's outlines, as marked at the end of what is written—Mrs. Lee has been in a state yesterday and today which makes me very uneasy. One of my children too is very unwell—and I have got a severe cold, attended with feverishness which makes all exertion painful.

Later he writes: "I am so unwell today, owing to a severe cold that I cannot write. I hope this will do for Monday. How to manage for examinations I do not know. Mrs. Lee is tolerably well again, but my little boy is very poorly." His son recovers, but Mrs. Lee continues to have periods of illness. These letters add a very human note to the lectures.

The lectures start with lecture 4 in the middle of a discussion on style. The first lectures covered elegance or beauty, and lecture 5 covers wit and imagination. Lecture 6 begins a course of lectures on logic. The first lecture (6) is dated January 9, 1821. He introduces this section by saying that, after "having taken a general survey of the capacities of the human understanding, we take notice of the important power of conveying our thoughts to one another by means of articulate speech, and we illustrate the principles of General Grammar" (lecture 6). He delineates as the great purposes of language "the communication of thought and the art of reasoning." He distinguishes rhetoric "as the art of pleasing or persuading" from the "more serious and useful art of logic." He uses the words *rhetoric* and *criticism* synonymously. He criticizes the practice where "in some Universities the lectures on logic have been superseded by lectures on Rhetoric and polite literature." He then lectures on sources of evidence from memory and testimony, moving to what he terms "dialectic," the art of reasoning. He considers in turn the syllogism, the enthymeme, induction, the methods of analysis and synthesis, and fallacies. He then covers Bacon's idols, or fallacies of the tribe.

After a series of lectures on "the Moral Faculty," the lectures that follow seem to be from a different course or courses after the lecture numbered 32. Lecture 33 is dated November 11, 1846, while the earlier lectures on logic are clearly dated 1821, the date when Dr. Lee held the chair of moral philosophy at King's College. (The same correspondence continues, and one wonders how many years the arrangement of sending his lectures to the long-suffering Alexander Simpson continued.)

These lectures are very difficult to read and sort out.

LEE, JOHN. 1820–21. EUL MS. Gen. Dk. 8.7–8. Unbound, unpaginated, tied in red ribbon in large box. Lectures are separated by binding and are numbered and dated. *Lectures on Rhetoric and Sermon Writing, 1821.* His own notes.

The first three bindings contain lectures on rhetoric, delivered on January 2, 3, and 4, 1821, presumably at Aberdeen where he held the chair of moral philosophy and logic from 1820 to 1821. He defines rhetoric as "that part of Intellectual Philosophy which professes to unfold the mode of communicating thought and feeling from one mind to another in a clear, impressive and pleasing manner" (January 2, 1821). He asserts that the discussion "is not less essential to the rules of strict argument than to the maxims of persuasive writing . . . it may be regarded equally as an introduction to Logic and to Rhetoric." He further defines rhetoric as

the Science which deduces from first principles and moulds into a system the rules we are subservient to in the beauty and excellence of composition. It is founded in a knowledge of the nature of man, and particularly in an acquaintance with Imagination, Taste and Passion. . . . All writers on the subject have drawn their rules from the practice of admired authors.

The idea of rhetoric as a "science" is repeated several times in these lectures. The following lectures treat three subjects: "the selection of words, the structure of sentences, and the skillful application of ornament" (January 3, 1821).

The next thirteen or fourteen bindings are lectures on sermon writing, delivered first in 1822, according to the date at the top, and used again in 1854 and 1856, according to the date on the spine, probably at the University of Edinburgh.

There is one undated lecture on aesthetics that carries the subject from Longinus through Kames, Gerard, Burke, and Blair. The final collection in the packet is an incomplete set of pages erratically numbered in a very careful handwriting, probably not Lee's. There is a section on imagination (87), on reason (99), and one on taste (103). Taste is defined as "that Power of the mind that enables us to perceive and to relish the beauties of nature and of art, and which renders us (in the language of a beautiful Poet) 'feelingly alive'" (103). The last section of these bindings, called part 4 (245), is "to point out the best method of communicating with clearness and precision to others the truths which we have discovered." This section is in a very careful handwriting, occasionally overwritten by a hand that resembles Lee's and may well be a student's notes. The lectures are entirely concerned with speaking and are undated.

There is a binding entitled *Lectures in Metaphysics and Moral Philosophy 1820*. A note on the title page reads, "Principal Lee seems to have taken Professor Wilson's course." Contrary to the note on the front, these lectures include an assortment of bindings dating variously from 1820, 1823, and 1857, including a lecture delivered in 1807 in London on the "Social Nature of Man." There are approximately eight bindings of lectures on moral philosophy dated 1820, which must have been delivered at Aberdeen. They appear to be largely concerned with logic and treat the usual subjects. The lectures do not follow each other and are very difficult to read.

SCOTT, HERCULES. 1821–60. AUL MS K. 196–197. 2 volumes: vol 1., 366 pp.; vol. 2, 733 pp. Writing clear, binding good. *Notes on Moral Philosophy from the Lectures of Dr. Scott. King's College. Aberdeen. 1848. Vol. 1 and 2. Taken by Geo. D. Bartlett.*
This set of so-called notes is made up of 1,205 questions, with their answers numbered consecutively. There are 990 questions under the heading of moral philosophy, 53 under the heading of law and jurisprudence, and 162 under the heading of evidences of Christianity. The questions seem to follow one another in subject matter. There is no way of knowing whether Professor Hercules Scott lectured in this manner or whether this is the work of an overly ambitious student; the title suggests the former.

Marischal College, Aberdeen: Moral Philosophy and Logic

GLENNIE, GEORGE. 1796–1840. AUL MS M 158. No title page and no date although the manuscript catalog dates this manuscript as 1812–13. Listed under Wm. Knight who took the notes. Text to p. 108 repeated in AUL MS M 206.
This manuscript contains three sections. The first section, psychology (1–243), contains an excellent, detailed table of contents at the end keyed to the numbered sections rather than to page numbers. The second section is entitled "Natural Theology," and the third section is "Moral Philosophy." The last

two sections are paged separately, although the numbered sections are continuous though not included in the contents. It is interesting to see that the bulk of these lecture notes concern the subject of psychology—now defined as the study of the human mind. Psychology is divided into two large parts: perceptive powers and active powers. Under perceptive powers are included consciousness (sections 52–98), attention (99–117), the faculty of speech (118–60), memory (161–74), imagination (175–87), the association of ideas (187–97), and dreaming (198–206).

Part 2, "The Internal Senses," after an introductory section contains sections on novelty (215–25), sublimity (225–32), beauty (233–42), imitation (243–57), harmony (251–52), ridicule (253–56), sympathy (257–61), and a concluding section on taste (261–63).

Another section, entitled the "Active Powers," includes sections on the will (276–80), instinct (280–85), habit (286–94), appetites, and a concluding section on the passions (296–332).

The second large division of this manuscript is entitled "Natural Theology" and explains what "human reason can discover concerning the being and attributes of God" (334–424). The last large division is entitled "Moral Philosophy" (sections 424–548), which is defined as that science that regulates "the active powers of man and contains rules for the improvement of his nature and for his attainment of happiness" (424) and as "the science that teaches man his duties and the reasons of it" (424).

GLENNIE, GEORGE. 1796–1840. AUL MS M 206. Vol. 1, 346 pp. (no vol. 2). Divided into numbered segments up to 200. Writing clear, binding fine. *Notes on Moral Philosophy and Logic Taken by Ernest Mearns. Marischal College. Aberdeen. Session 1812–13.*

These notes are an exact word-for-word duplication of George Glennie's notes contained in the first 108 pages of AUL MS M. 158. Taken by a different hand.

GLENNIE, GEORGE. 1796–1840. Course in Philosophy, 1834. EUL MS Gen. 850. 1 volume. Not paginated but lectures are numbered. Handwriting extremely difficult to read; much of the ink is faded. Binding poor, no front cover. *Lectures on Philosophy by Professor George Glennie, Marischal College, Aberdeen, 1834. Taken by William Simpson.*

This appears to be a very straightforward course in philosophy, with at least a third of the course devoted to a section entitled psychology and another section entitled "Powers of Perception by External Senses." After this section, the notes deteriorate, and the divisions are not clearly delineated.

This manuscript is very difficult to read; however, the tedium is relieved by the student's drawings—faces with noses of various sizes and shapes lining margins and heading pages of tiny handwriting. There are skulls also. On the back of the last page there is a cross-eyed Elizabethan and a lively fencing match in seven frames.

Toward the end of the notebook the student makes the following comment:

Tuesday—6th January 1835—(Morning)
This morning being seated in Dr. Glennie's classroom—the weather being excessively cold—etc. etc. I felt at a very great loss for something to do—Dr. Glennie was dictating fast enough in all conscience to keep twenty persons writing but I felt no inclination to be moral-philosophically engaged—

This comment is followed by a long peroration, with the heading "Students' Debating Society," concluding with a motion that a "Mr. William Ogg be expelled from that chair he has so unworthily filled." It is uncertain whether this is a real speech or whether it is the creation of a bored student who is having trouble keeping up with the dictation and who does not feel "moral-philosophically engaged."

MARTIN, WILLIAM. 1845–60. AUL MS U 524. No pages and no index or contents. Ink faded, binding disintegrated, and manuscript tied with a ribbon. *Moral Philosophy by P. J. Anderson. 1871–2.*

These notes were taken by the man who was later to become librarian and the prolific historian and keeper of the records of the university. This is the only set of Professor Martin's notes that we have.

Like most of his contemporaries, Martin starts his lectures by defining and classifying the sciences. He then goes on to define moral philosophy as examining "conscious voluntary action," inquiring into "causes, effects, or rules of action" (5). Moral philosophy examines the motives of human action. He maintains that, in general, philosophy asks and answers questions: natural philosophy asks a cause, intellectual philosophy asks a reason, moral philosophy asks a motive. Mental philosophy is divided into intellectual philosophy, which is logic, and moral philosophy. He continues in this manner, dividing and subdividing philosophy.

He then goes into a discussion of Sir William Hamilton and the British school of philosophy, with discussions of Locke, Berkeley, and Hume, followed by the Scottish school of philosophy of Reid. Martin includes no logic or rhetoric in this course.

Seth, Andrew (sometimes called Pringle-Pattison). 1887–91. EUL MS Gen. 1992/6. No date, no author. Three student notebooks on modern philosophy. The remainder of the box contains student notebooks on Scottish law. In pencil. Writing clear, but there are no page numbers or dates. *Modern Philosophy: II, Lectures 9–15; III, Lectures 16–22; IV, Lectures 23–31.*

Notes from the first eight lectures are missing, but from the rest of the lectures the course appears to be a rather ordinary course in philosophy, starting at lecture 9 with Francis Bacon and moving through René Descartes, Baruch Spinoza, Gottfried Wilhelm Leibniz, with the bulk of the later lectures devoted to Locke, Berkeley, and Hume.

The University of Aberdeen: English Composition and Rhetoric

Bain, Alexander. 1860–80. *Practical Essays.* London: Longmans, Green, and Co., 1884. 338 pp.

This is a volume of Bain's essays, mostly reprints of articles that have appeared in reviews. They range over a number of

162

the same time, England had only two institutions, and Scotland five. Among the basic needs of the colonists—aside from shelter and food—was the desire for schools. As the anonymous author of an early colonial treatise put it, "One of the . . . things we longed for, and looked after, was to advance *Learning* and perpetuate it to Posterity" (*New England* 12). In his history of Harvard University, Samuel Eliot Morrison states, "The two cardinal principles of English Puritanism which most profoundly affected the social development of New England and the United States were not religious tenets, but educational ideals: a learned clergy, and a lettered people" (45).

Many of these early American schools were little more than log cabins and dreams in the minds of their founders. Frederick Rudolph, the author of one of the definitive histories of American higher education, describes these early colleges: "Often when a college had a building, it had no students. If it had students, frequently it had no building. If it had either, then perhaps it had no money, perhaps no professors; if professors, then no president, if a president, then no professors" (47).

There were great difficulties in the new country. In Virginia the Crown allocated nine thousand acres in 1619 for the foundation of a college, but an Indian massacre in 1622 eliminated most of the institution's supporters. In 1693, the Crown granted a college charter to the state for "the saving of souls," but their majestie's attorney general reacted with the comment, "Souls! Damn your souls! Raise tobacco!" (11–15).

While the American universities were struggling for their existence in the early days of the eighteenth century, the Scottish universities were well established with a long history. The University of St. Andrews, the University of Glasgow, and the two colleges at Aberdeen were founded in the fifteenth century; the University of Edinburgh was founded in the seventeenth. There were no log cabins in the Scottish universities.

As early as the seventeenth century, education in Scotland had already begun to be considered both the right and the responsibility of every citizen. The educational system was built on a strong preparatory program of parish schools in the country and burgh schools in the cities. For a relatively poor country, Scotland had a well-established system of education. In the colonies, on the other hand, up until the Revolution in 1776, there was no provision for elementary education. Wealthier colonists provided tutors for their children, often Scottish tutors; but, for the most part, instruction in reading, writing, and arithmetic was the responsibility of the parents. But these parents had little time or energy for such pursuits. Life was hard for the early colonists.

With the widespread revival of religion in eighteenth-century America, the Great Awakening, congregations and churches split into a number of factions, into conservatives and liberals. The Congregationalists founded their own college, Dartmouth; then the Baptists and the Dutch Reformed followed suit. However, education in the colonies was still limited to the few largely because it was considered unnecessary for material success or for religious salvation. In 1775, it was estimated that only one of every thousand colonists had been to college, and most of those did not complete a full course. At the year of the Revolution, there were only three thousand living college graduates in the United States, many of whom became political leaders in the forming of the Constitution. Although some middle-class and lower-class families sent their sons to college, the "overwhelming majority of their sons stayed home, farmed, went West, or became—without benefit of a college education—Benjamin Franklin or Patrick Henry" (Rudolph 21–22).

In the eighteenth century, the American universities were still struggling. Rudolph tells a harrowing tale of the early years.

> On a cold drizzly day in January 1795, a two-story empty brick building that called itself the University of North Carolina was opened to the public. An unsightly landscape of tree stumps, rough lumber, scarred clay, and a bitter wind greeted the governor, who had wanted to be on hand for this important event. He was also met by the faculty which consisted of one professor doubling as president. A month later the first applicant for admission knocked at the door. In the same year, far to the north the founders of a college that would be called Bowdoin were offering the entirety of a township in Maine to any contractor who would build them a four-story building. They could find no takers. (47)

168

The history of Miami University, now one of the prestigious Ohio State Universities, tells the story of the Reverend John W. Brown and his efforts to raise money for the fledgling college. The president of the United States, James Madison, offered no assistance, but in Delaware, Brown raised twenty-two dollars, the president of Princeton gave him five dollars, and John Adams, in his retirement, gave him two books and ten dollars. Altogether, his efforts brought a wagonload of books and seven hundred dollars—a tremendous sum for the new college. Life was hazardous for the traveler in those days, though, and soon after his return, he slipped and drowned in the Little Miami River (Rudolph 44–45).

Fire took its toll on the early log buildings. Nassau Hall at Princeton burned, and the following year the first building erected at Dickinson College burned. At Ohio University, the only structure in existence was hit by lightning but was saved from total destruction by torrential rains (Rudolph 45). The spirit persisted. In 1842, eight French priests, barely able to speak English, walked into northern Indiana and founded the college that would become Notre Dame.

In spite of hardships, fires, and dissension, Americans never abandoned their dream of education. Two-thirds of the way through the eighteenth century, there were eight colleges. Between 1750 and 1800, twenty-seven American colleges were founded. By 1875, there were 250, of which 182 still survive.

There were only seven universities in the British Isles from 1591 to 1828, and Scotland had four of them. At the same time, more than seventy universities were founded in the United States that still survive. In the third quarter of the nineteenth century, in the red-brick explosion, the number of British universities doubled; during the same period in the United States, college enrollment also doubled.

Two events occurred in the 1800s that affected the North American universities. The first was the amassing of great fortunes by the robber barons, who in turn salved their consciences—and sometimes perpetuated their names—by founding colleges. Thus Vassar, Smith, Johns Hopkins, Stanford, Chicago, and Wellesley were all founded by individual donors. Although the states were unable to underwrite the number of private denominational insti-

169

tutions that had grown up, they were often able to give them land, of which there was still plenty in the nineteenth century. In most cases, sectarianism cut off state support and emphasized the private nature of these institutions. They increasingly looked to private donors for their support, just as they do today.

The second event of the nineteenth century that greatly affected the American institutions was the creation of land-grant colleges with the passage of the Morrill Act of 1862. Congressman Justin Morrill of Vermont, the man behind the legislation, suggested as early as 1848 that American colleges might well "lop off a portion of the studies established centuries ago as the mark of European scholarship and replace the vacancy—if it is a vacancy—by those of a less antique and more practical value" (Rudolph 249). Morrill introduced a bill in 1857 incorporating provisions for a technical and scientific education that, particularly in the case of agriculture, would deal effectively with the necessity for saving the resources of the land from erosion and soil depletion. The Morrill Act, passed in 1862 and expanded in 1887 with the Hatch Act, provided for a college in each state with studies related to agriculture and engineering, "without excluding other scientific or classical studies" (252). This act provided support for the state universities, some of which grew out of the small denominational colleges, some of which were combined with the private institutions (as at Cornell and Rutgers), and some of which were founded from the act. Out of the land-grant act came the great state universities of Michigan, Illinois, Ohio, Indiana, California, Minnesota, all of which now number well over fifty thousand students, and many of which, like California, have grown into huge state systems of ten or twelve interrelated institutions.

There was a similar development in Scotland in the initiation of evening classes in Glasgow in 1800 for working mechanics and artisans. In 1886, the various institutions that had arisen to provide technical education during the century were amalgamated into a single institution called Glasgow and West Scotland Technical College. In 1886, an agricultural department was added, but it was not until 1964 that it merged with the Royal College of Science and Technology to become the University of Strathclyde. In 1966, Heriot-Watt University was established in Edinburgh as a consolidation of a number of technical and scientific colleges. It

170

was out of the same impulse toward a technical, mechanical, and agricultural education that these institutions came into being and out of which the later universities developed. However, the movement was far less strong in Scotland and slower to develop than in the United States.

While the American universities in the nineteenth century were moving toward expansion to serve their population in an upwardly mobile society, which now equated a college degree with material success, the Scottish universities were embarked on reform. The Scottish universities were investigated by Royal Commissions, appointed in 1826, 1858, and 1876. After the 1707 Act of Union, Scotland had maintained its own democratic system of education, but with the 1858 Regulatory Act, the universities were nationalized. Standards were raised, entrance exams were instituted, and in so doing the Scottish universities lost their distinctive thrust and became, in effect, English. The ensuing acts of 1872 and 1889 completed the metamorphosis.

The Eighteenth Century: The Scottish Influence on America

In the eighteenth century, in contrast to the struggling American universities, those in Scotland were thriving. Free from the religious restrictions of the universities in England and Ireland, they attracted students from America and the Continent, as well as from England. Edinburgh's well-known medical school attracted many students from outside of Scotland. Moreover, it was at the Scottish universities rather than at Oxford or Cambridge that innovations took place. It was there that English literature as an academic study was introduced. Agriculture and Newtonian theories were added to the curriculum.

After the 1707 Act of Union, Scotland, freed of trade restrictions, prospered, and in the age of Enlightenment, the universities prospered as well. During the eighteenth century, Oxford and Cambridge on the other hand were a preserve for the "idle and rich." They were expensive and elitist and offered little that was new for the well-prepared student. The Scottish universities provided an education for the serious student from England and also drew students from the Continent and America. Their influence was broad, particularly in the United States.

There were a number of reasons for the strong Scottish influence on the philosophy, political thinking, and educational practices of the United States. Like the Americans, the Scots had always placed a high priority on education. Like the Americans, although the Scottish universities were primarily for the training of the ministry, the religious restrictions, particularly in the eighteenth century, were few compared to those at the English and Irish institutions. Like the Americans, the Scots believed in a practical education for their farmers and merchants. With certain deep philosophical beliefs in common, it was only natural that the early founders of the American universities looked to the Scots for their inspiration and for their leaders.

Scots and Americans both suffered from a colonial inferiority complex. The emphasis on education in the two countries and their ready acceptance of the concept of taste, as popularized by Hugh Blair, can be seen as an attempt to rid themselves of Scottish and American rusticisms and to become more "English." Both peoples spoke a nonstandard dialect, in that London English was the standard, and the rise of elocution teachers in both countries was a reflection of this lack of confidence not only in their own speech but in themselves as provincials. They also wished to understand literature—the entertainment of the upper classes before radio, television, and films. Reading aloud was an important part of elocutionary training; it was considered a tasteful activity and a decorous way for the well-bred family to pass their leisure.

At the same time, both Scotland and the United States experienced a revival in nationalism—Scotland in fear of losing its identity while taking on an English identity and the United States as a struggling new nation in the New World. Both countries were seeking a voice. Consequently, the United States was in many ways a fertile ground for Scottish influence during the eighteenth century. The skepticism of Berkeley and Hume had left the individual open to an unknown fate, and the Scottish philosophy of common sense was attractive to Americans in restoring their faith. In addition, Scotland and America shared a philosophy of government and education and a deep democratic bond that permeated their thinking and their actions. As a result, the exchange of peoples and ideas between Scotland and the United States proliferated. As Americans attended the world-renowned Scottish universities, Scots traveled in a steady stream to settle and work in the New World.

Many of the well-educated Scots entered the United States and established churches and presbyteries, offering the colonists the education they sought. Many found a place in religious institutions, in medicine, or in higher education. Others became schoolmasters or tutors. This migration was largely to the southern states—Virginia, Maryland, South Carolina, and Georgia. Some, however, went to Pennsylvania, particularly to Philadelphia, and a few to northern New York. Only a very few settled in New England. By 1790, there were between two hundred and two hundred fifty thousand people of Scottish birth or descent in the United States (Turnbull 137). William R. Brock demonstrates the difficulty of tracing Scottish Enlightenment thought in America, asserting that it may well be through the influence of these "hundreds of forgotten ministers, schoolmasters, tutors, and merchants" that Scottish ideas affected American thought, a fact that can be "neither measured nor ignored" (171).

Scottish educational philosophy permeated the early thinking in American politics and education. There was a deep philosophical bond between the Scots and the writers of the Declaration of Independence and the framers of the Constitution of the United States. Four of the signers of the Declaration of Independence were native-born Scots: Benjamin Rush, John Witherspoon, James Madison, and James Wilson. Archie Turnbull argues convincingly

> that the spirit that infuses many of the central doctrines of Congress, from 1774 to 1787, is in peculiar harmony with the legal, philosophical and moral teachings of Hutcheson, Reid and Kames; whose views in turn reflect the historical and constitutional inheritance of Scotland itself. Directly through their books, and as mediated by their disciples in the American colleges the ideas of these three men were familiar to all the most eminent statesmen, Franklin, John Adams, Dickinson and Jefferson among them. (149)

In his *Idea of a Perfect Commonwealth,* David Hume suggested that "areas be divided into communities of such a size that electors and representatives remained mutually aware of each other's needs and responses." Turnbull points out the striking similarity between Hume's ideas and the formation of the United States (Turnbull 149). He also emphasizes that Madison studied under John Witherspoon, who himself studied at Aberdeen, and Witherspoon's influence went far beyond his own students. He was active in the political issues of the day and was the only Christian minister to sign the Declaration of Independence. One of his colleagues during the 1777 Congress remarked about Witherspoon, "He can't bear anything which reflects on Scotland. The Dr says that Scotland has manifested the greatest spirit for liberty as a nation, in that their history is full of their calling Kings to account and dethroning them when arbitrary or tyrannical" (qtd. in Turnbull 144). This spirit infused the thinking in the early colonies and influenced political and educational decisions. In addition, many Americans went abroad to study at the highly respected Scottish universities. They then returned to become statesmen and educational leaders, bringing with them the Scottish democratic philosophy.

By far the greatest influence exerted by the Scots on the new nation was in education. Harvard College was founded in 1636, but the second college to be established in the New World was William and Mary in 1694. Its first president was James Blair, who had attended the grammar school of Marischal College in Aberdeen and had gone to the University of Edinburgh. He graduated from the arts program and then studied for the ministry. His Scottish career came to an end, however, when he refused to take the religious oath required by the Test Act of 1681 (Scott 205). On the founding of William and Mary College, he was appointed president for life. James Blair's heavy Scottish influence was evident in the system he set up—a grammar school or preparatory section, modeled on his own Aberdeen experience, and a philosophically based arts curriculum, followed by training in divinity. Students were accepted at an early age, as they had been in Scotland. He instituted specialized professorships, which were identical to those at Marischal and in direct contrast to the regenting system in operation at Harvard at the time (Sloan 20–21). Blair appointed many of his fellow Scots to positions in the college. Mungo Ingles, head of the grammar school, and Alexander Irvine, professor of natural philosophy and mathematics, were both Edinburgh graduates. He also appointed Dr. William Small from Marischal. Thomas Jefferson, one of the drafters of the Declaration of Independence, was one of Small's students and wrote admiringly in his *Autobiography* of his lectures on ethics, rhetoric, and belles lettres. He wrote of "habitual conversations" to which "I owed much instruction" (qtd. in Turnbull 140).

Francis Alison is a relatively neglected figure in the story of Scottish influence on American education (see McAllister; Turnbull). He studied under Francis Hutcheson, one of the early commonsense philosophers, at Glasgow, and student transcripts of Alison's lectures, which he gave at what would later become the University of Pennsylvania, were "Hutcheson *verbatim*" (Turnbull 140). William Smith, a graduate of King's College, Aberdeen, like Alison, first entered America as a tutor to the children of a New York family. In a series of pamphlets, he urged the founding of a college there, which would eventually become Columbia University. In 1754, he took a position teaching ethics, rhetoric, logic, and natural philosophy at the college that later became the University of Pennsylvania.

John Witherspoon, unlike Alison and Smith, went to New Jersey at the height of his career. He was forty-five years old and well known for his leadership in church affairs. He had written a number of religious pamphlets supporting the conservative cause, although he was primarily a mediator between opposing elements in the church. His concern for unity in the church was attractive to the Americans, who recruited him for the presidency of the College of New Jersey. He set up a curriculum with four classes that carried English names, *freshman, sophomore, junior,* and *senior,* but were a sequence of courses modeled after the Scottish universities. He introduced the Scottish method of dictating lectures, which were then used as a basic text. He lectured, continued as president for the college that was to become Princeton University, and maintained an active role in the political affairs of his day. He combined piety, politics, and rhetoric in his own career, but he is probably best known for his role in the American Revolution and as a signer of the Declaration of Independence. He brought to his career the rhetorical concept of the good man who is a good citizen. Michael Halloran speculates that English studies might have been greatly different if Witherspoon's lectures had received the wide circulation that Hugh Blair's *Lectures* had. Witherspoon's rhetoric was "a political art in the tradition of Aristotle and Cicero, an art of confronting civic issues" (Halloran, "Rhetoric and the English Department" 7).

The impact these Scotsmen had in the new colleges in America was strong and has been well documented, but the influence of hundreds of tutors and schoolmasters, though undocumented in the literature, may well have been equally strong. These individuals exerted an influence on the young people in the New World that was bound to have effects that long outlasted their own lifetimes.

In addition to this direct kind of influence, the indirect influence on American students exerted by the use of textbooks written by eighteenth-century Scotsmen was strong and remarkably long lasting. Hugh Blair's *Lectures* were published in Scotland in 1783 and were adopted as a textbook at Yale in 1785, at Harvard in 1788, and at Dartmouth in 1822. There were 130 editions of his *Lectures* in England and America, the last in 1911. Harvard still has on its shelves no fewer than twenty-six separate printings of the *Lectures* issued between 1789 and 1832. In 1850, it was used in twenty of forty-three American colleges and was in use at Yale and Williams until 1850 and at Notre Dame as late as 1880 (Kitzhaber 81). George Campbell's and Richard Whately's texts were also frequently used. Nan Johnson asserts that, in the first half of the nineteenth century, the rhetorical education of the average college student consisted mainly of studying Blair and Campbell and later Whately (19). The American universities were heavily influenced by the Scots both directly, through their teachers and educational leaders, and indirectly, through their reading, until the middle of the nineteenth century. It is not until then that America began to produce its own educational leaders and textbooks; and even during the second half of the nineteenth century, Bain's *English Composition and Rhetoric* was the most widely used textbook in American college English.

The Nineteenth-Century Connection

In the first half of the nineteenth century, the Scottish and American universities were similar in many ways. The American

176

universities were still based on the Scottish model. In the second half of the century, however, Scottish and American education took very different directions. Both were influenced by the German models in becoming graduate and research institutions; the American universities, like the English, felt the influence more than the Scottish. Johns Hopkins University was opened in 1876, and graduate education, based on the German model, was launched. The Scottish universities embarked on a series of so-called reforms in the second half of the century, and by 1900, as the American universities expanded, the Scottish universities adopted the English model, abandoning, in large part, their centuries-old philosophically based education.[1]

During the nineteenth century in Scotland, there were three distinct developments in the rhetoric courses, led by three outstanding educators at three quite different institutions: Edinburgh, Aberdeen, and Glasgow. In the case of Edinburgh, the development almost exactly paralleled the developments that were taking place at American universities. At Aberdeen, Alexander Bain developed a course specifically designed to improve the writing and speaking skills of the northern Scots, and his work was highly influential in the United States. In Glasgow, George Jardine prefigured many of the most important composition theories of the second half of the twentieth century in North America, but during the nineteenth century, he had little or no influence beyond his own university.

When William Edmondstoune Aytoun took over the chair of rhetoric and belles lettres at Edinburgh, the tradition of belles lettres was already well established. John Stevenson in the early part of the eighteenth century had lectured on English literature in his course in logic, metaphysics, and rhetoric. One of his students was Hugh Blair, who in 1759 took over the popular lecture series initiated by Adam Smith and Robert Watson in the city of Edinburgh. When the lectures were moved to the university, the chair of rhetoric and belles lettres was established. Aytoun held the chair from 1845 to 1865 and concentrated more and more on literature rather than on rhetoric. At the beginning, examples from English literature were used to demonstrate principles of rhetoric, but gradually the analysis of literature became the focus of the course, an emphasis vastly preferred by both the professor and his students. In 1860, Aytoun received the English literature chair. At approximately the same time, Francis Child at Harvard initiated the study of English literature in the United States. It was first designated as a field of study in 1868–69, and the trend at Harvard was fairly typical of what happened at other schools in the United States (Kitzhaber 34).

Largely because of the success of Aytoun's course at Edinburgh, the Royal Commission in 1861 recommended that the study of English be instituted at all of the Scottish universities. But for the students in the north, the study of English, under Alexander Bain, was not the study of literature; it was the study of grammar and composition. His psychology students idolized him; his English students abhored his course. His widely used text, *English Composition and Rhetoric*, initiated the idea of the paragraph as an important division of discourse marked by unity, coherence, and emphasis, as well as the topic sentence, the thesis, and other concepts still familiar to millions of American students. That book was also the most widely used text in North American universities in the second half of the nineteenth century (Johnson, Appendix). Bain has been vilified by the composition theorists, who attribute to him the worst of the current traditional rhetoric practices. He deserves more study to exonerate him; these charges are largely undeserved. Bain, in fact, takes much of the blame for didactic rules established by the later text writers who adapted his work. The fact remains, however, that Alexander Bain, through his textbook, exerted a strong and direct influence on the American composition course.

While Bain's small textbook had numerous editions and was widely influential in the United States, George Jardine's book *Outlines of Philosophical Education* (first published in 1818) was reprinted only once, in 1825. Bain's ideas were eagerly adopted in both Scotland and the United States, while Jardine was largely ignored after his own lifetime. His pedagogical theories are surprisingly similar to those of contemporary compositionists. He used peer evaluations, sequencing of theme assignments, collaborative learning, and class discussions. He suggested encouragement for the beginning writer and overlooking "first faults" and saw writing as a process and as discovery. Even the terms in which he states his theories sound amazingly like the compositionist

Commission in 1858, the field was broadly conceived. English included some history, a little geography, and a literature that encompassed essays in history, science, and philosophy. Today, literature has narrowed its scope to include only what David Masson considered "literature of the imagination," only a quarter of his course. Scientific and historical essays were once part of the canon, but today such essays find their place only occasionally in the freshman composition course.

One obvious change, apparent throughout the nineteenth-century courses, is the shift of rhetoric as a generative, creative act to rhetoric as an interpretive, analytical act. Over and over in these course notes we find rhetoric being defined as "criticism." Robert Eden Scott asserted that the "science" of rhetoric was "also sometimes denominated [as] Criticism, Eloquence, or the Belles Lettres" (AUL K. 190–191).

The same kind of mental shift took place in music and the other arts, as scholars interpreted and criticized music, art, and literature rather than producing it. The reasons for this reformation are open to conjecture. It is easier and far more pleasant to criticize than to create, as anyone who has put pen to paper or brush to canvas can attest. The rise of the universities during this period certainly further encouraged this shift as a canon of English literature was established and scholars sought new ways to look at an ever-narrowing body of material.

The shift from a generative rhetoric to an interpretive rhetoric is never complete in the nineteenth century, so that professors of English maintain their interest in and emphasis on composition while concentrating their efforts, with the exception of Alexander Bain, on literature. In nineteenth-century rhetoric, literature and composition are bound together for better or worse.

The wedding between composition and literature was consummated by economic factors in the second half of the nineteenth century, when the German influence ushered in the large graduate programs that dominated the American and British universities for the next century. It proved to be a happy economic union for composition and literature in the North American universities but an increasingly unhappy philosophic one. Composition courses were turned over to graduate students. Professors were relieved of the onerous duty of teaching writing and reading themes and could devote their time to the study of literature. Literary scholar-ship thrived; rhetoric and composition scholarship at the univer-sity level languished. Only education schools maintained any inter-est in composition theory or pedagogy.

For North American administrators, the arrangement was economically advantageous. The largest course in the university, the only required course for every student, was taught with cheap labor. Once established, there was no way to reverse the situation without a large outlay of money. For English professors, the situation was even more propitious. The composition course sup-ported their Ph.D. students who, in turn, filled their Milton and Shakespeare seminars, so that they could continue to teach the subjects that interested them. Graduate students, however, found teaching composition a burden only vaguely related to their study of literature. Sometimes it was made tolerable for them by the introduction of some literature. Or they sneaked in a bit of *Sartor Resartus* in their freshman course since they had just covered it in their graduate seminar. The graduate students in the 1940s and 1950s, forced to teach writing while pursuing their studies in literature, came to despise it. When they graduated and found jobs in the expansion of the sixties, they thankfully took up teaching in their individual literary specialties, gratefully turning composition over to graduate students, vowing never to teach it again if they could help it. One of the lures to attract promising new faculty was the pledge that "they would never have to teach composition." The unhappy wedding of composition and literature continues to the present day. Even the flooding of the market with English literature Ph.D.s, unable to acquire positions, failed to alter a situation too firmly entrenched and too satisfying to administra-tors and English literature professors. In the 1970s and 1980s, graduate programs in rhetoric/composition came into existence—within English departments—more as an answer to the job market than as a philosophic change. Most of these programs, however, still emphasized literature, either through required course work or through the shape of the comprehensive exams. English professors still wanted to fill their Milton seminars.

Belletristic composition, as conceived by Hugh Blair, as encouraged in the 1960s by the expressive school of Peter Elbow, Donald Murray, and Ken Macrorie, as locked in for financial reasons in the twentieth century, is firmly in place by the end of the twentieth century. Because of the job market, graduate programs in rhetoric/composition attract students, many of whom in reality vastly prefer studying literature. Students in literature programs display rhetoric prominently in the titles of their dissertations in order to enhance their chances in the ever-tightening job market. As a result, composition texts, for the most part, are strongly belletristic, urging students to find a voice, to search for an identity, to explore meaning, and to write in metaphor and simile. The American composition course celebrates the personal and exploratory essay and is more concerned with stylistic niceties than persuasive arguments about issues. Students are urged to read and write literature, and more and more the composition course is losing its classical basis in a rhetoric that explores public issues and encourages informed opinions. The belletristic trend was introduced in the nineteenth century and continues in the twentieth, encouraged by irreversible economic and political factors. Having grown up and shared its youth with literature, criticism, and psychology in the house of eighteenth- and nineteenth-century Scottish rhetoric, composition comes by its belletristic bent naturally.

One can only speculate about what the twenty-first century holds. One change that is already occurring is the enlargement of the canon. English literature is being expanded as the writings of African-Americans, Hispanics, Asians, and women are added. An interesting fact is that these writings often do not follow the established modes of canonical writings. New genres, such as letters and diaries, are being investigated as writings outside of the patriarchal canon are being discovered and appreciated.

Another change already under way came when engineering, agriculture, business, and journalism schools found their students less and less able to mount an argument or organize a paper. It was out of this realization that the writing-across-the-curriculum programs were established in North American universities. And with them came the perception that the subject matter of rhetoric could be anything from a chemistry experiment to a math problem, and more important, that anyone who wanted to do so could teach writing. So finally, in the American universities, writing might become the responsibility of every professor as it has been and still is in Britain and western Europe. In the century to come, writing-across-the-curriculum programs may finally free rhetoric/composition from the English literature departments—a not altogether unhappy solution. In turn, the huge glut of English literature Ph.D.s might finally be mitigated. Composition might return to its original rhetorical basis of civic issues and informed judgments. In such an academy, rhetoric/composition might take its place as a legitimate scholarly area in its own right and be freed of its Cinderella role in the English literature department. And students might then learn how to mount an argument or analyze an issue and be citizens in the fullest sense of the rhetorical ideal.

This study has been an effort to explore the past, to trace the roots of English literature, criticism, and belletristic composition in nineteenth-century Scotland. In this investigation of the past, perhaps we may better guide and direct our future.

Notes
Works Cited
Index

⚚ | *Notes*

Preface

1. It was through the bibliographies of James R. Irvine and G. Jack Gravlee in the *Rhetoric Society Quarterly* (vol. 8:4; vol. 10:1; vol. 13:1) that I first became aware of the seventeenth- and eighteenth-century materials in Scottish archives.

1. The Missing Link

1. For the historical background for this period in Scotland, see R. D. Anderson, *Education*; for a study of nineteenth-century Scottish education and the resistance to English encroachment, see the study by George Elder Davie, *Democratic Intellect*.
2. Many of these lectures have been reprinted in facsimile in the Southern Illinois UP Series, *Landmarks in Rhetoric and Public Address*, edited by David Potter.
3. All citations to archival materials appear exactly as listed on the manuscripts and therefore vary. They are further identified by their library abbreviations: EUL, University of Edinburgh Library; GUL, University of Glasgow Library; AUL, University of Aberdeen Library; NLS, National Library of Scotland. The professors' manuscripts whom I quote are listed chronologically in the annotated bibliographies.
4. The best readily available record that we have of Aytoun's lectures is the book by Eric Frykman, which includes excerpts from his lectures, his letters, and his reports to the Royal Commission. His lectures have not been published, probably because he was constantly altering and rewriting them. The manuscripts for his lectures on rhetoric are in the National Library of Scotland: NLS MS 4897, 4909–11.
5. The calendars at the Scottish universities are the equivalent of the American university bulletins. The early calendars have detailed course descriptions and are available in the Scottish university libraries. And, although not published until the second half of the nineteenth century, they are a readily available source of information for that period.

189

2. The Background

1. There is much recent and excellent scholarship on the Scottish Enlightenment. See especially Sloan; Sher; and Daiches, Jones, and Jones.
2. This influence has been well documented, particularly in a collection of articles in *Scotland and America in the Age of the Enlightenment*, edited by Richard B. Sher and Jeffrey R. Smitten (Princeton, NJ: Princeton UP, 1990).

3. Eighteenth- and Nineteenth-Century Schools and Universities: Rhetoric and Composition

1. Hans sets out in his work, *New Trends in Education in the Eighteenth Century*, to refute the commonly held view of Oxford and Cambridge in the eighteenth century—especially the view that the poor students had deserted the universities—but his arguments are not always convincing against the greater evidence to the contrary.
2. *The Rhetoric of Blair, Campbell, and Whately*, edited by James L. Golden and Edward P. J. Corbett (Carbondale: Southern Illinois UP, 1990), provides excerpts from the works of these rhetoricians with an updated bibliography. The authors' excellent introduction gives a good account of the eighteenth century and the way in which these rhetoricians reacted to their own times. Probably the excerpts in this volume, first published in 1968 (New York: Holt), were the first introduction to Scottish rhetoric for many students. Wilbur Samuel Howell, in *Eighteenth-Century British Logic and Rhetoric* (Princeton, NJ: Princeton UP, 1971), also gives a detailed account of Campbell's *Philosophy* and a not altogether flattering account of Blair's *Lectures*, "the most popular and the most influential, but not the most meritorious" of the rhetorics of the new age (648).
3. According to Henry W. Meikle, "Hugh Blair borrowed his [Smith's] notes and followed his master so closely that he was accused of plagiarism" (91). Smith requested that his lectures be burned on his death, which some scholars take as further proof of Blair's plagiarism. However, we now have student notes from Smith's lectures (Bryce and Lothian), and there is little evidence for the charge. Smith was strongly opposed to the practice of dictating and would not allow his students to take down his lectures word for word. The one set of notes that we have appears to be a reconstruction of his lectures by two students working together after the lecture (Bryce). A more reasonable explanation for his request that his lectures be burned is that he did not wish students to get hold of them.

4. Women were not included in the democratic ideal. It was not uncommon for women to attend the parish and burgh schools, but since the purpose of higher education was to train persons for the church and state, and since women were generally excluded from those professions, a university education was not considered important. In 1865, women were admitted to examinations at Edinburgh, but it was not until 1892 that the Scottish universities awarded degrees to women.

4. The University of Edinburgh

1. We know a great deal about student life at the University of Edinburgh through the writings of and about Thomas Carlyle. See Ian Campbell; David Masson; and the works of Carlyle, himself.
2. Two excellent sources of information on the study of English literature and the establishment of the Regius chair at the University of Edinburgh are the article by Henry W. Meikle, "The Chair of Rhetoric and Belles Lettres in the University of Edinburgh," *University of Edinburgh Journal* 13 (1945): 89–103; and the manuscript entitled "Rhetoric and Belles Lettres" in box 2 of the Horn papers, EUL Ms. Gen. 1824.
3. Two of Greenfield's colleagues, one in medicine and a specialist in mental diseases, argued that Greenfield suffered from "appetitive insanity" and should be dismissed "without ignominy" (Horn 7). One cannot help but wonder.
4. Aytoun's changes are made in ink. The penciled changes and comments, according to the librarian at the NLS, were made by Sir Theodore Martin when he perused the manuscripts while writing his *Memoir of William Edmondstoune Aytoun* (London, 1867).
5. It is interesting that his contemporary, Francis Child, the first English literature professor at Harvard, also collected ballads and, like Aytoun, is best known today in the United States for that work. I can find no record that either man knew the other or that they were even aware of their mutual interests.

5. The University of Glasgow

1. Lynée Gaillet has written an important dissertation on George Jardine (Texas Christian U, 1991) in which she demonstrates the many ways in which he prefigures the work of modern composition theorists.
2. I can offer no explanation for this quotation from the *Dictionary*. The article is signed by "R.M.W." and is taken in part from memoirs by Veitch's niece, Mary R. L. Bryce.

7. The Scottish-American Connection: The Emergence of Belletristic Composition

1. George Elder Davie, in *The Democratic Intellect: Scotland and Her Universities in the Nineteenth Century* (Edinburgh: Edinburgh UP, 1961), gives a lively account of this change during the nineteenth century. He defends the Scottish philosophy-based university education and regards the visits by the Royal Commissioners as "assaults" on Scottish education. It was this book that originally piqued my interest in the Scottish-American connection during this period. R. D. Anderson's later book, *Education and Opportunity in Victorian Scotland: Schools and Universities* (Oxford: Clarendon P, 1983), offers a clear, well-documented view of what he calls the Scottish universities' adaptation "to the changing conditions of the nineteenth century" (361).

2. It was, of course, almost always *English* literature. Scottish and American literature did not enter the academy as legitimate studies until well into the twentieth century. It proved as difficult for these native literatures to find their places in the universities as it had been for English literature.

✍ | Works Cited

Allan, A. "Autobiographical Notes." U of St. Andrews Manu-
scripts.
Alma Mater. University of Aberdeen Magazine, 21.3 (October
14, 1903).
Anderson, P. J. *Aurora Borealis Academica: Aberdeen University
Appreciations 1860–1889.* Aberdeen: U Printers, 1899.
———, ed. *Studies in the History and Development of the University.*
University of Aberdeen Studies 19. 1906.
Anderson, R. D. *Education and Opportunity in Victorian Scotland:
Schools and Universities.* Oxford, Clarendon P, 1983.
———. *The Student Community at Aberdeen 1860–1939.* Quincen-
tennial Studies in the History of the University of Aberdeen.
Aberdeen: U of Aberdeen P, 1988.
Archer, R. L. *Secondary Education in the Nineteenth Century.* Cam-
bridge: Cambridge UP, 1921.
Arnot, Hugo. *History of Edinburgh.* Edinburgh: Creech and Mur-
ray, 1779.
Aytoun, William Edmondstoune. National Library of Scotland.
MS. 4897, 4913.
Bain, Alexander. *Autobiography.* New York: Longmans, Green,
and Co., 1904.
———. *A Companion to Higher English Grammar.* London, 1874.
———. *English Composition and Rhetoric, A Manual.* London,
1866.
———. *A Higher English Grammar.* London, 1872.
———. *Mental and Moral Science.* London: Longmans, Green,
and Co., 1872.
———. *Practical Essays.* Longmans, Green, and Co., 1874.
Barnard, H. C. *A History of English Education from 1760.* 2d ed.
London: U of London P, 1961.
Bator, Paul. "The Formation of the Regius Chair of Rhetoric and

Belles Lettres at the University of Edinburgh." *Quarterly Journal of Speech* 75 (1989): 40–64.

Blair, Hugh. *Lectures on Rhetoric and Belles Lettres.* Ed. with an introduction by Michael Halloran and Greg Clark. Carbondale: Southern Illinois UP, 1992.

Bower, Alexander. *The Edinburgh Students' Guide: Or an Account of the Classes of the University.* Edinburgh, 1822.

Braddock, Richard. "The Frequency and Placement of Topic Sentences in Expository Prose." *Research in the Teaching of English* 8 (1974): 287–302.

Brock, William R. *Scotus Americanus: A Survey of the Sources for Links between Scotland and America in the Eighteenth Century.* Edinburgh: U of Edinburgh P, 1982.

Bryce, J. C. "Introduction." In *Adam Smith's Lectures on Rhetoric and Belles Lettres,* ed. A. S. Skinner. Indianapolis: Liberty Classics, 1985.

Campbell, George. *The Philosophy of Rhetoric.* Ed. with an introduction by Lloyd Bitzer. Carbondale: Southern Illinois UP, 1989.

Campbell, Ian. "Carlyle and the University of Edinburgh." In *Four Centuries of Edinburgh University Life,* ed. Gordon Donaldson, pp. 53–71. Edinburgh: U of Edinburgh P, 1983.

———. *Thomas Carlyle.* New York: Scribner's, 1974.

Carlyle, Thomas. *On the Choice of Books.* London, 1866.

Comrie, J. D. *University of Edinburgh Journal* 17 (1953–55).

Connors, Robert J. "The Rise and Fall of the Modes of Discourse." *College Composition and Communication* 32 (1981): 444–55.

Court, Franklin E. "The Social and Historical Significance of the First English Literature Professorship in England." *Publication of the Modern Language Association* (1988): 796–808.

Daiches, David, Peter Jones, and Jean Jones, eds. *A Hotbed of Genius: The Scottish Enlightenment 1730–1790.* Edinburgh: U of Edinburgh P, 1986.

Davidson, William Leslie. "The University's Contribution to Philosophy." *Studies in the History and Development of the University.* University of Aberdeen Studies 19, ed. P. J. Anderson, pp. 73–97, 1906.

Davie, George Elder. *The Democratic Intellect: Scotland and Her Universities in the Nineteenth Century.* Edinburgh: U of Edinburgh P, 1961.

in the Age of the Enlightenment. Princeton, NJ: Princeton UP, 1990.

Sloan, Douglas. *The Scottish Enlightenment and the American College Ideal.* Teachers College, Columbia U: Teachers College P, 1971.

Stewart, Donald C. "Some History Ideas for Composition Teachers." *Rhetoric Review* 3 (1985): 134–44.

Stone, Lawrence. "Literacy and Education in England, 1640–1900." *Past and Present* 42 (1969): 69–139.

Turnbull, Archie. "Scotland and America, 1730–90." In *A Hotbed of Genius: The Scottish Enlightenment,* eds. David Daiches, Peter Jones, and Jean Jones, pp. 137–52. Edinburgh: U of Edinburgh P, 1986.

University of Edinburgh Journal 17 (1953–55).

Vickers, Brian. *Classical Rhetoric in English Poetry.* New York: St. Martin's, 1970.

Watson, Robert. "Heads of Lectures on Rhetoric and Belles Lettres." MS Dc. 6.50/2. Edinburgh University Library.

Official Publications (in chronological order)

Report Made to His Majesty by a Royal Commission of Inquiry into the State of the Universities of Scotland (1831) (PP 1831, xii).

Evidence, Oral and Documentary, Taken and Received by the Commissioners . . . for Visiting the Universities of Scotland; vol. 1: *University of Edinburgh* (1837) (PP 1837, xxxv); vol. 2: *University of Glasgow* (1837) (PP 1837, xxxvi); vol. 3: *University of St. Andrews* (1837) (PP 1837, xxxvii); vol. 4: *University of Aberdeen* (1837) (PP 1837, xxxviii).

First Report of the Commissioners Appointed . . . for Visiting the Universities of King's College and Marischal College, Aberdeen (1838) (PP 1837/38, xxxiii); *Second Report* (1839) (PP 1839, xxix).

Report by the Commissioners Appointed . . . for Visiting the University of Glasgow (1839) (PP 1839, xxix).

Report of the St. Andrews University Commissioners (1845) (PP 1846, xxiii).

Report of Her Majesty's Commissioners Appointed to Inquire into the

State of the Universities of Aberdeen, with a View to Their Union (1858) (PP 1857/8, xx).

Scottish Universities Commission. General Report of the Commissioners Under the Universities (Scotland) Act, 1858. With an Appendix (1863) (PP 1863, xvi).

Report to the Royal Commissioners Appointed to Inquire into the Universities of Scotland, with Evidence and Appendix; vol. 1: *Report with Index of Evidence* (1878) (PP 1878, xxxii); vol. 2: *Evidence—Part 1* (1878) (PP 1878, xxxiii); vol. 3: *Evidence— Part 2* (1878) (PP 1878, xxxiv); vol. 4: *Returns and Documents* (1878) (pp 1878, xxxv).

Report to the Commissioners under the Universities (Scotland) Act, 1889, as to the Subscription of Tests by Principals, Professors, and other University Officers in the Scottish Universities, vol. 1 (n.d.) (PP 1892, xlvii); *Appendix to the Report of the Commissioners under the Universities (Scotland) Act, 1889, as to the Subscription of Tests . . .* , vol. 2 (n.d.) (PP 1892, xlvii).

General Report of the Commissioners under the Universities (Scotland) Act, 1889. With an Appendix (1900) (PP 1900, xxv).

Index

151; influence of, 8, 11, 38; treatise of empiricism by, 27
Logic (*see also* Rhetoric *and individual professors*), 8, 10, 38, 41, 50, 53; definitions of, 8, 85, 88, 91, 116, 117, 120; at King's College, 141–44; and literature at University of Aberdeen, 141, 146, 148–49; at Marischal College, 144–48; and psychology, 12, 13; at St. Andrews, 134–36; at University of Edinburgh, 60, 61, 68–69; at University of Glasgow, 94, 97, 105, 107, 117
London University, 66, 136, 137
Lothian, John M., 30
Lunsford, Andrea, 147

McCormick, William Symington, 134, 136, 137–38
McCosh, James, 27, 28
McLachlan, 43
Macrorie, Ken, 184
Madison, James, 169, 173, 174
Marishal College (*see also* Aberdeen, University of), 19, 26, 49, 140, 149, 150; professors of, 40, 140–41, 142, 144–48; students of, 12, 38, 49, 174. *Archival materials:* 159–62
Martin, William, 125, 142, 161–62
Masson, David, 7, 48, 56–57, 60, 137; archival materials on, 75–83; elements of courses taught by, 66, 182–83; teaching methods of, 44, 66–67
Medicine, 37, 49, 51, 133, 171
Medieval education, 18–20, 40
Meikle, Henry W., 61

Melville, Andrew, 19, 21, 22, 95–96
Mental and Moral Science, a Compendium of Psychology and Ethics (Bain), 11
Miami University, 169
Michael, Ian, 41, 48
Miller, Thomas P., 166
Milton, John, 66
Minto, William, 141, 142, 148
Modern Language Association, 2
Moir, George, 60, 62, 63, 71–72
Moral philosophy (*see also* Logic; Rhetoric), 12, 50, 141–42, 150–52, 160, 162
Moral sense (*see also* Commonsense philosophy), 28
Morgan, Alexander, 20, 21
Morrill, Justin, 170
Morrill Act, 170
Morrison, Samuel Eliot, 167
Munro family, 44
Murphy, James J., 1
Murray, Donald, 179, 184

National Church of Scotland, 17, 24
Nationalism, 32, 33, 172, 182
National Library of Scotland, 63
Navigation Acts, 16
New Jersey, College of, 175
Newton, Sir Isaac, 5, 27, 49, 88, 151
Nichol, John, 97, 107–8, 125–29
Nineteenth-Century Rhetoric in North America (Johnson), 165
Norman Sinclair (Aytoun), 64
North Carolina, University of, 168
Notre Dame University, 10, 169, 176

Winifred Bryan Horner is the Lillian Radford Chair of Rhetoric and Composition at Texas Christian University. Her publications include *The Present State of Scholarship in Historical and Contemporary Rhetoric* (revised edition), *Rhetoric in the Classical Tradition,* and *Composition and Literature: Bridging the Gap.* She has written extensively and presented a number of papers on composition and rhetoric and on her Scottish research.

Her work has been supported by the University of Edinburgh Institute for the Humanities and by the National Endowment for the Humanities. In 1982, she received an award from the University of Missouri for outstanding contributions to the education of women and was honored as a distinguished alumna in 1990. A festschrift in her honor, edited by Theresa Enos, is forthcoming from Southern Illinois University Press. She has presented papers at universities in Amsterdam, Aberdeen, Cottengen, Edinburgh, Oxford, Tours, and Shanghai. She served as president of the National Council of Writing Program Administrators and the Rhetoric Society of America. Her contributions to the field of composition and rhetoric and her role as a scholar, teacher, and mentor have been noted by her colleagues in works such as "Three Heroines: An Oral History" by Sharon Crowley (*PRE/TEXT* 9 [1988]) and *Growing Up Female in Composition: Lessons in Power, Lessons in Weakness,* forthcoming by Sally Harrold and Jeane Harris.

The present book is the result of her many years of research on nineteenth-century Scottish rhetoric.